INDIANA'S FAVORITE RESTAURANTS

REID DUFFY

Indiana's FAVORITE RESTAURANTS

WITH A RECIPE SAMPLER

INDIANA
UNIVERSITY
PRESS

Bloomington and Indianapolis

This book is a publication of
Indiana University Press
601 North Morton Street
Bloomington, Indiana 47404-3797 USA

www.indiana.edu/~iupress

Telephone orders   800-842-6796
Fax orders   812-855-7931
e-mail orders   iuporder@indiana.edu

*The paper used in this publication meets
the minimum requirements of American
National Standard for Information Sciences
—Permanence of Paper for Printed Library
Materials, ANSI Z39.48–1984.*

MANUFACTURED IN THE UNITED STATES OF AMERICA

Library of Congress Cataloging-in-Publication Data

Duffy, Reid.
    Indiana's favorite restaurants : with a recipe
sampler / Reid Duffy.
        p.   cm.
    Includes index.
    ISBN 0-253-21439-4 (pa : alk. paper)
    1. Restaurants—Indiana—Guidebooks.
2. Cookery.   I. Title.

TX907.3.I35 D84 2001
647.95772—dc21
00-047260
1 2 3 4 5   06 05 04 03 02 01

Contents

Introduction   vii

Indiana's Favorite Restaurants   1

COMFORT FOODS   77

WHERE'S THE BEEF?   96

ETHNIC EATING   103

DESTINED TO STAND THE TEST OF TIME   116

Index   135

Introduction

During my more than two decades of reviewing and writing about the dining scene in Indianapolis, statistics have continued to proclaim that 85 to 95 percent of our nation's restaurants either close or change ownership within five years of opening their doors. To be sure, not all of these changes represent failure, but enough of them do to reflect the precariousness of this particular industry where, to customers, you are only as good as the last meal you served them.

The primary purpose of this book is to acquaint you with some Hoosier restaurants that have truly stood the test of time, maintaining a level of quality, service, and consistency that spans generations, and often with intriguing stories to tell. In several cases, they started as small, unpretentious diners with seemingly modest prospects and ambitions, only to be found two to four decades later as dining behemoths blithely serving hundreds of customers a day, many arriving by chartered bus.

Their formula has been to whip up meals just about any Hoosier will enjoy (and as you'll see, skillet-fried chicken and chargrilled hunks of red meat are good places to start). Cook it as best you can, as consistently as you can, and be on the premises to make sure it is done and served the way you want it done and served. This relatively simple formula is remarkably difficult to pull off on a day-to-day basis, for all sorts of reasons.

In this book we showcase 30 Hoosier restaurants, trying to give you a feel for what makes them great and throwing in some of their favorite recipes along the way. (We present them as they were presented to us in terms of portions served, leaving it up to the reader whether to cut down [or increase] the ingredients. We did edit them for consistency of style, and when necessary listed the ingredients in order of use.) We then follow that with a section on our favorite comfort food palaces, ethnic eateries, and relatively young restaurants that have made very good impressions and are destined to stand the test of time. I write this with the expectation of being taken to task by readers about worthy Hoosier restaurants not included in this tome, because I wasn't sure, or was unaware, or simply forgot. We welcome your thoughts about this, and hope to include your candidates in subsequent editions the publisher is no doubt confident will come to pass. Bon appétit!

REID DUFFY

INDIANA'S FAVORITE RESTAURANTS

Acapulco Joe's Mexican Restaurant
INDIANAPOLIS

365 N. Illinois St.   (317) 637-5160

Open Monday–Thursday 7 A.M.–9 P.M.; Friday–Saturday
7 A.M.–10 P.M.; closed Sunday except on Colts home game
days 11:30 A.M.–8 P.M.

Eight times a day, customers at Acapulco Joe's in downtown Indianapolis will be jolted into respectful silence by Kate Smith's
invigorating rendition of "God Bless America," played at a jukebox
volume of Mach 12, in tribute to the restaurant's founding father,
Joe Rangel—for nearly 30 years Indianapolis' most colorful dining
impresario.

"God Bless America" meant and spoke volumes for Joe, born in
1925 to a large, impoverished family in a small Mexican farming
community. As a teenager, Rangel left his hometown for the land
of opportunity just across the Rio Grande. Six crossings resulted in
six deportations back to Mexico. His seventh attempt got him as
far north as Springfield, Missouri—and an all-expenses-paid, nine-
months' stay at the federal penitentiary there, having annoyed U.S.
Immigration officials once too often. A fellow inmate suggested he
marry an American woman to ease his pursuit of U.S. citizenship,
and he duly lined up a woman 20 years his senior who was willing
to accept his proposal.

Predictably, this May-December match did not hold up, but
it allowed Joe to establish a foothold in Texas, maintaining a low
profile as he made his way on foot, at night, from Brownstone to
Corpus Christi over a seven-day stretch. There he formally entered
the American restaurant industry as a bus boy at a Greek restaurant.
Told of a waiter's job at a Mexican restaurant in Minneapolis, several thousand miles away from the southern division of the U.S.
Border Patrol, Rangel saved up $40 for the one-way bus trip. How-
ever, the ticket agent could have sworn Joe said "Indianapolis," and
that is where the bus deposited him.

Rangel quickly found odd jobs in Indy, and so impressed a local druggist named Joe Felsher with his industry and ambition that Felsher loaned him $5,000 to purchase a small, rundown diner on the southwest corner of Illinois and Vermont streets. Rangel spruced up the premises, and in 1960 Acapulco Joe's opened for breakfast and lunch as what is believed to be Indianapolis' first Mexican restaurant. It was soon attracting a breakfast crowd seeking to jumpstart their day with Joe's spicy Mexican omelettes and hearty sausage and gravy, while long lines around the block paid tribute to the lunch menu with its well-seasoned, creatively cheesed tacos, enchiladas, burritos, tamales, and chile con queso. Adding to the reputation was Joe's penchant for kidding, kibbitzing, and pontificating with male customers and flirting with female customers as he cooked, and for hiring attractive waitresses garbed in "hot pants," at that time a compelling fashion statement.

Felsher's loan was paid back quickly, with interest in the form of a nearly daily flow of chili, stews, and turkey from a deeply appreciative Rangel, until Felsher urged him to stop in the interest of dietary restraint. 1971 marked another major milestone in Rangel's American odyssey when he achieved his dream of becoming a U.S. citizen. The sign out front declared, "Hear ye! I, Joe Rangel, became a U.S. citizen. Now I'm a proud Gringo and can raise hell about taxes like any other citizen. Come in and share my bliss." Those who accepted the invitation no doubt were greeted with another high-volume rendition of "God Bless America" to punctuate the grand moment.

In 1984, Acapulco Joe's moved across the street to roomier quarters at the southeast corner of Illinois and Vermont when American United Life Insurance commandeered his little café to make room for an employee parking lot. But Joe found that the tripled seating capacity and a kitchen separated from his customers cramped his style and challenged his ability to provide prompt and efficient service. Still, the lines continued to snake around the corner at lunchtime. Gradually, Joe trained others to do the bulk of the cooking, while he worked the room with his magic tricks and Kate Smith singalongs, introducing newcomers to his infernal Mexican wombat, housed in a cage that would suddenly snap open, scaring the curious and gullible out of their intimate apparel, followed by relief tinged with embarrassment upon learning the cage contained only a fake-fur tail.

Joe Rangel died in 1989, and his family sold the business to his longtime cook, Raymond "Butch" Phillips. Phillips was able to maintain Acapulco Joe's culinary standards, but became overwhelmed by the business aspects, creating tax and debt problems that nearly closed the restaurant for good. Enter one of Joe's closest friends, Bob McNeil, an Indianapolis policeman looking for a career change. Attacking the fiscal problems with gusto, he got Acapulco Joe's back on a sound financial footing. In the process, McNeil may have created the safest restaurant in Indiana: many of his former colleagues breakfast and lunch there in full uniform to fuel up for another interesting day in the Indy urban tapestry.

And in honor of the founder, whose framed photograph looms over the restaurant in spiritual quality control, McNeil and Phillips dutifully summon Miss Kate to belt out "God Bless America." It is the number-one hit on the jukebox. The number-two hit also gets plenty of air time, for it was Joe Rangel's second favorite song, summing up his life as he saw it and lived it: "The Impossible Dream."

JOE'S TACO FILLING

1½ pounds ground beef
1 teaspoon crushed red peppers
1 teaspoon minced garlic
1 teaspoon black pepper
1 teaspoon ground cumin seed
1 pinch oregano

1 tablespoon tomato paste
1 teaspoon salt
1 tablespoon beef base
2 cups flour
½ cup catsup
¼ cup tomato sauce

Add ground beef, spices, tomato paste, and beef base. Cook 10 minutes. Add the flour to the meat (do not drain beef). Cook 10 minutes. Add catsup and tomato sauce. Cook for 5 minutes.

JOE'S HOT SAUSAGE GRAVY

1 pound Rudy's brown sausage
1 tablespoon crushed red peppers
1 pinch salt
1 pinch black pepper

1 pinch ground cumin seed
1 cup flour
½ gallon 2% milk

Brown sausage thoroughly. Add seasonings. Cook 5 minutes over medium flame. Add flour to sausage mixture. Blend well. Add milk and stir with wire whisk. Add more milk to desired thickness. Best served over hot biscuits.

Beef House
COVINGTON

I-74 and State Road 63   (765) 793-3947

Open Monday–Friday 8 A.M.–10 P.M.,
Saturday 2:30–10:30 P.M., Sunday noon–9 P.M.

In the early 1960s, Covington businessman Warren Wright was raising cattle when, one day at the supermarket, he noticed beef was selling for around $1.50 per pound while he was receiving 20 cents off the hoof after caring for and feeding the source. This realization inspired Mr. Wright to begin sharpening his beef grilling skills, winning kudos at various 4–H Fairs for his charcoal rib-eye cook-outs.

According to Wright family lore, Warren's foray into the restaurant business came about as the result of an organ transplant. In hopes of encouraging musical pursuits among his five offspring, he purchased an expensive organ for the parlor. When he noticed it gathering dust he announced that he was sending it back and opening a restaurant instead. And so he did, in 1964, purchasing a relatively modest café in Covington, installing and firing up a charcoal grill, and introducing his hefty rib-eyes, T-bones, porterhouses, and New York strips to an appreciative throng. His wife, Ellen, familiar with her husband's penchant for thinking big and following through, pitched in with her homemade noodles and grand finale pies. Soon the Beef House, perched as it was just a few miles east of the state line, was attracting practicing carnivores from Illinois as well as Indiana.

Bob Wright was the only one of their quintet of children who could be talked into continuing the Wright dining legacy. He allowed himself to be lured from Purdue upon his 1967 graduation, undaunted by the fact that his degree was in veterinary science. Bob and his wife Bonnie came armed with a recipe from Purdue's hotel-restaurant management school for huge, doughy dinner rolls that became an instant Beef House trademark, even as these mutant rolls threatened customers' appetites for a big juicy steak.

In 1975, Bob Wright figured it was time to spread out, and he created a beefier 500-seat Beef House off I-74 at the Newport/Lebanon/State Road 63 exit, perched on a hill three miles west of Covington and four miles east of the Illinois border. A few years later, the Wrights built a separate 500-seat banquet hall upon noting that every area high school sports team, service organization, and other group with a desire to make their annual dinners and meetings memorable, at least for the food, was booking the Beef House early and often.

At the front entrance of the main restaurant, customers are greeted with a glass case display of beef cuts, from which they can personally select if they find a T-bone with their name on it. And they can monitor the cooking of that steak over white-hot charcoal in the open kitchen. The Wrights estimate they grill 3,500 to 4,000 pounds of beef a week for approximately 7,500 customers showing up each week for all three meals. Fresh seafood, chicken, and pork chops round out the menu.

Bob and Bonnie's three children, Brad, Greg, and Sarah, appear poised to carry on, secure in the knowledge that their clientele will not lose their taste for beef on the charcoal grill, and that their late grandfather Warren's conclusion about which is more profitable, supply or demand, was correct.

BEEF HOUSE BROCCOLI SOUP

½ gallon water
½ cup chopped carrots
½ cup chopped onions
¼ cup chopped celery
¼ pound butter, melted
3 teaspoons flour

1 teaspoon black pepper
1 pound American or cheddar
  cheese
1 pound chopped broccoli
1 pint half-and-half
1 quart milk

Bring water, carrots, celery, and onions to a boil. Mix melted butter and flour until smooth. Stir into boiling mixture, then add pepper and cheese. Stir until cheese has melted. Then add the broccoli. After boiling for 2 minutes, add the milk and half-and-half.

BEEF HOUSE BLEU CHEESE DRESSING

3½ gallons mayonnaise
3 quarts half-and half
½ cup cracked black pepper

3 pounds bleu cheese wheel
2½ pounds crumbled bleu cheese

Mix all the ingredients together and refrigerate overnight.

Café Johnell
FORT WAYNE

2529 S. Calhoun St.   (219) 456-1939

Open Tuesday–Saturday 6–9 P.M.

Café Johnell in Fort Wayne ranks as Indiana's most consistently honored and nationally acclaimed restaurant, boasting four stars from the prestigious *Mobil Guide* and ongoing praise for its French and continental cuisine and its elegant, pampered service from such lifestyle arbiters as *Holiday, Esquire, Gentlemen's Quarterly, Playboy, Wall Street Journal,* and *Chicago Tribune,* plus assorted national and international restaurant associations. It has been a most intriguing odyssey for a dining institution that began life in 1958 as Big John's Carry-out.

What Big John's customers were carrying out back then were barbecued ribs and chicken from the grill of John Spillson, situated in a former ice cream stand at the corner of Calhoun and Woodland streets on Fort Wayne's gritty southside. The next year, it became Big John's Pizzeria—one of the earliest in Fort Wayne. In 1960, Spillson's tiny establishment grew with his lofty ambitions, expanding to a full-service Italian restaurant appropriately called Johnelli's. The following year, Spillson blithely flicked the "i" from Johnelli's to give his restaurant, now known as Café Johnell, a decidedly French accent, with a menu that featured Dover sole, coquilles Saint-Jacques, prime beef, veal, rack of lamb, and roast duck.

Spillson did not make these transitions on a whim. He was weaned on the restaurant business. His Greek-born father, Nick, and three uncles owned and operated prominent Fort Wayne restaurants, most notably the popular Berghoff Gardens, throughout the '30s and '40s. John's stint in the merchant marine during World War II took him to many European ports of call where, in off hours, he would visit the most prominent restaurants and apprentice himself to the great chefs in order to learn what made their kitchens and dining rooms prosper.

As he gradually and carefully entered the precarious restaurant business, Spillson noted the dawn of the Kennedy administration and the lavish media attention being paid to Jacqueline Kennedy's cultural tastes, which inspired an escalation of classy French restaurants in New York, Chicago, and San Francisco. He took pains to visit the more notable of these and pick the brains of the chefs and proprietors.

So by the time he formally opened Café Johnell on January 13, 1961, Spillson was able to hit the ground running, aided by his wife, Jayne, an interior designer, who created lush, royal red European drawing-room decor for the three primary dining areas and elegantly adorned them with Old Master paintings, in stark contrast to the restaurant's squat, nondescript exterior that harked back to its neighborhood ribs-and-pizza roots. Meanwhile, Spillson developed a wine cellar equal to the cuisine, and, with earthy showmanship, would place a laurel wreath on his dome as Fort Wayne's official representative of Bacchus, god of wine and good times.

As Café Johnell's reputation soared, the Spillsons sent their daughter, Nike (pronounced "Nicky") to France to be educated at the fabled Cordon Bleu cooking school. She then apprenticed under prominent chefs in Paris and later New York. It took a while for John to lure his daughter away from the charms of Paris and New York, back to Fort Wayne, to show off what she had learned. But it was worth the trouble. Nike's return further elevated the creativity and presentation of the continental dishes, from the whole Dover sole in Bearnaise sauce to the pastry-encrusted beef Wellington, and the national acclaim continued.

With Jayne Spillson's death in 1986 and John's passing in 1995, Nike took over full ownership of Café Johnell, enhancing the decor with impressionist paintings and three-dimensional "toile" paper sculptures that showcase a typical Café Johnell repast. Like her father, Nike has resisted urgings that she move Café Johnell to more upscale environs downtown or to the northside, or even to Indianapolis. In the spirit of "don't fix what ain't broke," she keeps complications to a minimum by concentrating on simply providing the exquisite dining experience that is the 90-seat Café Johnell, with its lush cuisine, plush ambience, and lavish hospitality and service, where—in response to a customer's request to "doggy bag" his unfinished filet—a server, instead of depositing it in a styrofoam container, may slice it thin, dab on mustard or another sauce, insert between two slices of rye bread, and present as a sandwich for the late-night dining enjoyment of the customer or his pooch. And that is how Fort Wayne finds itself on the national dining map.

CHICKEN LIVER PÂTÉ

1 pound chicken livers
3 envelopes gelatin and ¼ cup cold water
1 tablespoon chicken base
1 tablespoon Dijon mustard
3 dashes Lea & Perrins steak sauce
1 dash Tabasco sauce
1 pinch thyme
1 cup port
2 sticks softened butter, in small pieces
1 cup heavy cream

Boil water and poach chicken livers; drain. Soak gelatin and add the chicken base, dijon mustard, Lea & Perrins sauce, Tabasco, and thyme. Place in blender with the chicken livers and purée. Add port and butter to the blended ingredients. When smooth, add the cream and pour into oiled pâté mold. Refrigerate one day, to set up, before unmolding.

GRAND MARNIER SAUCE

1 cup sugar
5 egg yolks
1 cup heavy whipping cream
¼ cup Grand Marnier

In a double boiler, using a hand mixer, cream together yolks and sugar. Beat until tripled in volume, pale yellow in color, and forming a ribbon. Remove from heat and stir in ½ the Grand Marnier. Allow to cool. Whip cream, folding in custard mixture and remaining Grand Marnier. Refrigerate.

Chanteclair
INDIANAPOLIS

5th Floor, Airport Holiday Inn
2501 S. High School Rd.   (317) 243-1040

Open Monday–Saturday 5:30–10 P.M.

When brothers Bob and Jim Dora opened their Holiday Inn at the Indianapolis International Airport in 1968, they assumed the hotel dining room would be a conventional forum for steaks and seafood. They were surprised and skeptical when hotel manager Fred Davis suggested putting a high-ticket French restaurant on the hotel's 5th floor. The brothers Dora wondered whether an expensive French restaurant would be the proper fit for a hotel whose national reputation and marketing revolved around its budget-friendly room rates. But Davis figured that the bulk of their clientele would be road-warrior businessmen needing a place to wine and dine clients in a manner that would impress them with their impeccable style and their bountiful expense account.

So the Doras gave their blessing, and Mr. Davis recruited flamboyant French-born maitre d' Gigi Pecon and respected continental chef Hubert Schmeider to get Chanteclair off the ground. At the time, there was a dearth of such fine-dine emporiums in Indianapolis, let alone at its airport. Pecon and Schmeider were able to recruit many of the gifted waiters from the Keys on North Meridian Street when that fondly remembered restaurant closed its doors. Chanteclair survived its inevitable growing pains, and began to hit its stride in the mid-'70s when Austrian-born Dieter Puska entered the Chanteclair kitchens after a productive apprenticing stint at the renowned Maisonette in Cincinnati. His delicately sauced veal, beef, lamb, and fresh seafood dishes quickly established Chanteclair as one of the city's premier restaurants for classic French and continental cuisine, most notably the Dover sole, beef Wellington, and tableside preparation of the flame-provoking Steak Diane.

On the weekends, Chanteclair became a more provocative place as innumerable locals gathered to celebrate life's various milestones, including marriage proposals and escalations of romantic relationships, over chateaubriand, crèpes Suzette, and cherries jubilee for *deux*. There was even a strolling violinist to punctuate the moment with the proper melody of passion.

Puska left in the early '70s to open the Glass Chimney in Carmel. But his successors, most notably Matt Wise, kept Chanteclair's reputation lofty. Jim Dora took the same approach to high-class sustenance at the Holiday Inn Holidome which he opened off 1-465 and North Michigan Road in 1979, with its Italian-accented fine-dining restaurant, San Remo (872-3434). With Jim Dora and his Holiday Inns, continental goes well beyond breakfast.

STEAK DIANE

2 pounds center-cut beef tenderloin, in ½ inch slices (12 pieces)
4 ounces sliced mushrooms
4 chopped shallots

3 cups Bordelaise sauce (see below)
1 ounce brandy
3 tablespoons clarified butter

Bordelaise sauce:
6 teaspoons butter
½ cup diced onions
4 tablespoons flour
2 cups beef bouillon, homemade or canned

½ cup red wine
1½ tablespoons chopped parsley
2 cloves garlic, crushed
1 tablespoon Dijon mustard
2 tablespoons heavy cream

Bordelaise sauce: Heat butter in large skillet. Sauté onions in butter until golden. Add flour and blend thoroughly. Add bouillon and stir until smooth. Blend in wine, parsley, and garlic. Add mustard and heavy cream.

Steak Diane: Heat large skillet over medium heat. Add clarified butter and sauté the beef tenderloin strips, searing on both sides. Add mushrooms and shallots. Sauté until tender. Add Bordelaise sauce. Add brandy to the skillet and heat thoroughly. Serve immediately.

CAESAR SALAD (serving 4 to 6)

¼ teaspoon pepper
2 cloves garlic, peeled and chopped
3 to 4 anchovies
1 lemon, cut in half
1 tablespoon Dijon mustard
dash Worcestershire sauce
1 coddled egg (placed in shell in boiling water for 1 minute)

½ cup salad or olive oil
2 tablespoons red wine vinegar
1 head Romaine lettuce, washed, drained, torn, and patted dry
1 cup croutons
1 cup Parmesan cheese, grated

In wooden bowl, combine pepper, garlic, and anchovies. Then squeeze in the juice of half a lemon. Mash together until a paste is formed. Add the mustard, Worcestershire sauce, and coddled egg. Gradually add oil to the mixture and whisk until the dressing thickens. Add red wine vinegar and stir. Add Romaine lettuce, croutons, and Parmesan cheese. Then squeeze other lemon half on top. Toss and serve in chilled salad dishes.

Chez Jean
CAMBY

State Road 67, 20 minutes southwest of
downtown Indianapolis   (317) 831-0870

Open Tuesday–Saturday 6–10 P.M.,
Sunday brunch 11 A.M.–2 P.M.

For Hoosier devotees of classic French cuisine and gracious dining, Chez Jean has been the quintessential destination restaurant ever since 1957, when French-born Jean Milesi opened his charming country French bistro off State Road 67, near Mooresville.

Milesi was born to a family well versed in the culinary arts, with several siblings and relatives becoming chefs in the classic French tradition. Young Jean joined an older brother in Louisville, Kentucky in 1953 where he got some American fine-dining experience. Three years later, he was just about to follow his culinary muse to California when he learned of a small motel–burger and chicken operation up for sale on State Road 67, just 20 minutes from downtown Indianapolis. The eatery (a former turkey barn) and 12-room motor lodge, in a country setting surrounded by pine trees, fit Milesi's needs and bankroll. With some remodeling, Jean fashioned a winsome bistro to showcase his delicately sauced roast duck à l'orange, rack of lamb, coquilles Saint-Jacques, coq au vin (chicken in burgundy wine–mushroom sauce), Dover sole in lobster bisque cream sauce, veal sweetbreads, and such stirring finales as dessert soufflés, baked Alaska, crèpes Suzettes, and other traditional *classiques Française* not previously seen in those parts.

Shortly afterward, Jean met and married his wife, Barbara, who not only served as a gracious waitress but lent her stylish touch in adorning the motel rooms with antiques, fresh flowers, and other winsome garnishments designed to convince their clientele of the romantic potential of Chez Jean. And that is how Chez Jean became central Indiana's most distinctive setting in which to celebrate anniversaries, birthdays, budding relationships, and getaway romantic interludes, with the Milesis operating on their long-expressed theory that Chez Jean is a place one goes not to eat, but to dine . . . to be pampered, not to be rushed. On an educational note, Chez Jean has been the object of a culinary field trip by virtually every high school French club in the area.

Jean and Barbara Milesi decided to retire in the mid-'90s, turning Chez Jean over to their son, Thomas, who operated the restaurant briefly before deciding to pursue other ventures. At that point, the Milesis turned to old friends—a much-honored chef, Carl Huckaby, and his wife, Leva—who formally took over Chez Jean in February 1997. Huckaby had been a chef at several Indianapolis-area restaurants and country clubs, but developed an early relationship with chef Jean as owner of a nearby bakery that supplied Chez Jean with French breads and rolls. Being devout customers, the Huckabys found it easy to emulate the light Milesi touch. At the same time, they have brought a few muscular Huckaby triumphs to the table, such as stuffed veal, prime rib with roast garlic, grilled pork chops, salmon, and tuna, breaded orange roughy sautéed in almonds and amaretto, and a bountiful champagne Sunday brunch.

Beset by health problems in the late '90s, Jean and Barbara passed away within a few months of each other in 1999, just as the Huckabys' son, Carl, Junior, an accomplished chef in his own right, joined his parents in the kitchen, helping to establish a family dining legacy while paying tribute to the memory of the dining legend who brought French traditions to the Hoosier heartland.

PORK TENDERLOIN MEDALLIONS WITH WHITE COGNAC CREAM SAUCE, MORELS, AND LOBSTER

20–24-ounce true pork tenderloin
fresh morels
2–3 ounces lobster meat (slipper, langostino, or medallion)

cognac
bechamel sauce of flour, butter, and milk

Using a true pork tenderloin (with the tenderness of fish), remove all silver, skin, etc., and cut into ½ inch medallions. Using 4 to 5 medallions, the weight of each should be 5 to 6 ounces. Grill medallions to medium, taking care not to overcook.

Meanwhile, lightly sauté fresh morels in a skillet. (Reconstituted dry morels, squeezed dry, can be substituted.) Add lobster meat. Deglaze skillet with cognac and add the traditional bechamel white sauce.

Serve the white cognac sauce with lobster over the medallions of pork tenderloin.

CRÈME BRÛLÉE

pinch salt	6 egg yolks
½ cup sugar	vanilla
1 tablespoon cornstarch	1 pint heavy cream

Dry-mix salt, sugar, and cornstarch. Blend in egg yolks, and then add vanilla and heavy cream. Pour into shallow oven-proof custard dishes (single-serving size). Bake at 350° with water bath until set (after about 35–45 minutes). Let cool, then top lightly with equal parts brown sugar and granulated sugar. Caramelize the sugar under broiler or with torch. Garnish with dollop of whipped cream and fanned strawberry. Serve immediately while warm.

Das Dutchman Essenhaus
MIDDLEBURY

240 U.S. 20   (800) 455-9471; (219) 825-9471

Open Monday–Thursday 6 A.M.–8 P.M.,
Friday–Saturday 6 A.M.–9 P.M.

When Bob and Sue Miller opened their restaurant on U.S. 20 in Middlebury in January of 1971, it was in a pleasant one-story, L-shaped brick structure with seating for 120 and a staff of 24. As it entered the new millennium, it had blossomed into a virtual kingdom—Das Dutchman Essenhaus, Indiana's largest restaurant—prepared to handle as many as 1,100 customers in one sitting on two sprawling levels, with a staff of 450, a bakery, and a country-crafts gift shop that meanders around the spacious dining rooms upstairs and down.

In the heart of Indiana's Amish country, 20 miles east of the South Bend–Elkhart area, it would seem at first blush an unlikely spot for such an expansive operation. But the locale was just what the Millers had in mind when they moved to Middlebury from Sugarcreek, Ohio, also an area with notable Amish and Mennonite populations, and where tourist destinations were created by tapping into the Amish lifestyle with its country cooking and deceptively simple, exquisite crafts. Sensing such a business opportunity in northern Indiana, the Millers set up stakes in a mobile home on the property, at the 24-hour truck stop they bought in 1970 on U.S. 20.

Old-timers remembered that the spot was once home to an eatery called the Curve Inn, situated a tad too close to a major bend of the road, which resulted in more than a few accidents when inattentive drivers plowed into the building. The Curve Inn was eventually destroyed by fire, and was replaced by Everitt's Highway Inn, poised a bit more discreetly back off the road, catering to truckers and motorists around the clock, and enjoying a brisk Sunday trade with fried chicken and apple pie dinners. After the Millers bought the restaurant, closed it for a week to decorate, and then opened for business as Das Dutchman Essenhaus, the first thing regulars noticed was that the cigarette machine had been escorted from the premises. The second thing was that it was no longer open on Sundays, out of respect to the cadre of Amish and Mennonite women hired to whip up their tried-and-true country recipes.

Locals had grave doubts about its prospects, since it was not inclined to take on what appeared a natural constituency—the potentially lucrative after-church crowd. But doubts tended to evaporate when they made the acquaintance of the Essenhaus broasted chicken and roast beef, served family style with legitimate mashed potatoes and gravy, home-style dressing and noodles, and home-baked bread and apple butter. They also discovered that those ladies in the kitchen knew a little something about making and baking pies guaranteed to cause a high degree of diner rapture . . . from fruit to cream pies, with shoofly pie in between.

Before long, tour buses full of eagle-eyed shoppers heading for the fabled flea markets of nearby Shipshewana were pulling up; the menu had expanded to include ham, pork chops, roast turkey, meat loaf, chicken pot pie, and nearly 30 pie selections; and the restaurant was open for all three meals.

And thus it came to pass that the Essenhaus became a full-blast destination restaurant, where on its busiest days, with many banquets, it might serve 8,000 customers and bring joy to its suppliers of staples. According to their statistics, Das Dutchman each week goes through 300 pounds of salt; 2,800 pounds of white sugar; 7 tons of potatoes; 1,400 dozen eggs; 4,100 chickens; 5,300 pounds of roast beef; 4,000 heads of lettuce; and 40,000 napkins.

The Millers purchased an adjoining farm to increase their land holdings to over 100 acres, and renovated and converted several old buildings on the premises into the artsy-crafty Essenhaus Village Shops, including a petting zoo. A 33-room Essenhaus Country Inn was added in 1986, and Essenhaus Foods was created to produce and market the Millers' salad dressings, noodles, and bakery items.

With sons Joel, Jeff, and Lance Miller and son-in-law Randy Yoder providing second-generation leadership, Das Dutchman Essenhaus has 50 more acres available to develop additional country-fresh attractions, and to continue its mission as Amish country's most compelling tourist destination.

APPLE DUMPLINGS
(from Das Dutchman Essenhaus Amish Country Cookbook, Vol. 1)

6 medium-sized baking apples

2 cups flour
2½ teaspoons baking powder
½ teaspoon salt
⅔ cup shortening
½ cup milk

Sauce:
2 cups brown sugar
2 cups water
½ cup butter
¼ teaspoon cinnamon or nutmeg
(optional)

Pare and core the apples, and leave in halves. To make the pastry, sift flour, baking powder, and salt together. Cut in shortening until particles are about the size of small peas. Sprinkle milk over mixture and press together lightly, working dough only enough to hold together. Roll the dough as for pastry and cut into 12 squares.

Place half an apple on each square. Fill the cavity in each apple with sugar and cinnamon. Wrap dough around apple to cover it completely. Fasten edges securely on top of apple. Place dumplings one inch apart in a greased baking pan.

Combine brown sugar, water and spices. Cook 5 minutes, then remove from heat and add butter. Pour sauce over dumplings. Bake at 375° for 35–40 minutes, basting occasionally. Serve hot with rich milk or ice cream.

BISCUITS

2 cups sifted flour	2 tablespoons sugar
2 teaspoons baking powder	$\frac{1}{2}$ cup shortening
$\frac{1}{2}$ teaspoon cream of tartar	1 egg
$\frac{1}{2}$ teaspoon salt	$\frac{2}{3}$ cup milk

Sift dry ingredients together and cut in shortening. Pour milk in slowly.

Add egg and stir. Knead on lightly floured surface. Pat or roll into $\frac{1}{2}$ inch thick portions and place on baking sheet. Bake for 10–15 minutes at 450°.

Dodd's Townhouse
INDIANAPOLIS

5694 N. Meridian St.   (317) 257-1872

Open for lunch Tuesday–Friday 11:30 A.M.–2:30 P.M., dinner Tuesday–Saturday 5–8:30 P.M., Sunday 11 A.M.–8 P.M.

Dodd's Townhouse, in the historically prosperous Meridian-Kessler neighborhood of Indianapolis since 1962, traces its roots back to World War II when Betty Dodd collaborated with her father-in-law, Claude Dodd, to open a small diner called the Chick-Rib across the street from an amusement park called Little America at 62nd and Keystone. Betty's husband, Jim, was serving in the Army Medical Corps, and Claude, a printer by trade, was looking for a career change. Back then, a journey to 62nd and Keystone was still considered a drive to the country, and well worth the gas coupons for the Dodds' commendable repertoire of chicken, ribs, and pie.

When Jim returned from the Army, the family decided to expand by taking their country dining deeper into the country, to the cornfields of 120th and North Meridian—to Carmel in its pre-suburban period—and in 1948 came the debut of Dodd's Flagpole Restaurant, with its signature flag pole outside, which quickly proved to be a big attraction for area farmers. The problem was, mostly they would just sit a spell over a five-cent cup of coffee, whiling away the afternoon complaining about the weather, low farm prices, high taxes, and politicians. Betty soon felt compelled to double the price of coffee to ten cents to discourage the java squatters and make room for serious diners who were prepared to take on fried chicken and skillet-grilled steaks with chasers of buttermilk and apple pie. (The Flagpole was also one of the first Hoosier restaurants to offer baked potatoes on a consistent basis).

After 14 years in Carmel, the Dodds moved to their current location at Meridian and Westfield Boulevard, to a log house built as a residence in the early 1900s by Albert and Polly Alice Carter. Throughout the late '40s and '50s, the building had housed a series of family-style restaurants, one of them with the elegant moniker Meridian Street Chicken House. It had been called the Homestead just before the Dodds assumed command, when it became Dodd's Flagpole Towne House, ultimately streamlined to Dodd's Townhouse.

With its move back into the city, Dodd's steaks seemed to take center stage, with imposing filets, rib-eyes, and New York strips grilled on the cast-iron skillet, creating a crusty exterior to lock in the juices. The pan-fried chicken still enjoys specialty status, especially when served family style to larger groups, with bowls of mashed spuds and gravy, green beans, corn, slaw, and ice cream.

Most of Dodd's devout customers refuse to leave the premises without a generous slice of flaky-crusted pie, diet or no diet, whether it be the seasonally adjusted cherry, apple, peach, blueberry, or blackberry or the calorically charmed chocolate cream, banana cream, coconut cream, or buttermilk pie. Even when Jim and Betty Dodd glided into retirement mode after turning the restaurant over to son David and his bride, Rita, in 1978, they still maintained quality control over the pies, Jim taking over the engineering of the pie crust and Betty in charge of the enriched filling. The Dodds' involvement in the pie-making process continued almost up to the time of Jim's death in 1998.

David Dodd now superintends the cast-iron grill and Rita supplies the charm as hostess in the cozy 100-seat main dining room (there is additional seating for 25 in an upstairs room). Children Jamey, Erin, and Danielle are poised to take over when needed.

CHOCOLATE CHIP PIE (for 2 pies)

2 cups sugar
¾ cups flour
8 ounces melted butter
4 eggs

1¾ teaspoons vanilla
2 cups chocolate chips
2 cups chopped nuts

Mix well and pour into 2 unbaked pie shells. Bake one hour at 300°.

BUTTERMILK PIE (for 3 pies)

7 eggs (well beaten)
4 cups sugar, saving one
   cup for the flour
2½ tablespoons sifted flour

2½ teaspoons vanilla
1¼ cups melted butter
2½ cups buttermilk

Mix extremely well and pour into 3 unbaked pastry shells. Bake 45 minutes at 375°.

Foxfires
MUNCIE

3300 Chadam Lane (off McGalliard Road [State Road 332])
(765) 284-5235

Hours: Monday–Saturday, 5 P.M.–11 P.M. Closed Sunday

After Garfield the Cat achieved superstar status in the comic sections of 2,500 newspapers, his creator, Muncie cartoonist Jim Davis, found himself meeting with assorted producers, publishers, agents, and company heads seeking to generate television specials, books, and novelty products. They would trek to Davis's estate outside of Muncie, but when it came time to seal the deal over dinner in the manner to which they were accustomed, they would have to travel to Indianapolis to find the upscale restaurants considered appropriate to the occasion.

Since there was nothing in Muncie to fit Mr. Davis's burgeoning business dining needs, he purchased Foxfires in 1984 and turned the conventional steak and seafood restaurant launched by supermarket magnate Don Marsh in the late '70s into a fine-dining mecca that draws many gourmands from Indianapolis. To assuage regulars from the previous administration, Davis essentially created two restaurants under its one roof, one of them, in the bar area, featuring steaks, chicken, fresh seafood, pasta, and bar cuisine.

The main dining room, with its soft-toned contemporary decor and a splendid glassed-in view of Foxfires' extensive wine selections, serves as a forum for a seasonally changing menu of innovative American cuisine, encompassing goose liver and goat cheese appetizers, prime beef, stuffed veal and pork chops, roast duck, lamb loin, venison, fresh seafood, and even ostrich. The husband-and-wife team of executive chef Jeffrey Carrigan and general manager Amanda Carrigan preside over the restaurant, with Mr. Davis, a knowledgeable connoisseur of the grape, taking a personal hand in developing the prized wine list.

Jim Davis frequently displays the paintings of local artists in the restaurant, with his own striking oil paintings of his prime meal ticket, Garfield, in all the feline's smirking splendor, adorning the main dining room. Incidentally, Garfield's favorite dish, lasagna, does not appear on Foxfires' menu—perhaps a subtle act of independence by his creator.

RUM-MANGO GLAZED PORK CHOPS

3 tablespoons olive oil	2 teaspoons curry powder
4 tablespoons shallots, minced	1 cup fresh mango juice
2 teaspoons fresh garlic, minced	$\frac{1}{2}$ cup rum
1 teaspoon ground cumin	2 cups pork or chicken stock
1 teaspoon freshly ground	3 tablespoons molasses
black pepper	6 pork chops, 10 ounces each

Heat oil in a saucepan over medium heat; add shallots and garlic; sauté until golden. Add spices; sauté for 3 minutes. Remove from direct heat; carefully stir in juice and rum. Return to heat; add stock; bring to a simmer.

Stir in molasses; reduce to a glaze (about 30 minutes); remove from heat and cool.

Brush pork chops with glaze; refrigerate for at least 2 hours. Grill to desired doneness.

SMOKED SALMON CHEESECAKE (serves 12)

1 cup freshly grated Parmesan cheese
1 cup bread crumbs
$\frac{1}{2}$ cup unsalted butter, melted
1 tablespoon olive oil
1 cup chopped onions
$\frac{1}{2}$ cup chopped green bell peppers
$\frac{1}{2}$ cup chopped red bell peppers
2 teaspoons salt
12 turns freshly ground black pepper
3 tablespoons chopped fresh dill
$1\frac{3}{4}$ pounds cream cheese, room temperature
4 large eggs
$\frac{1}{2}$ cup heavy cream
1 cup grated smoked Gouda cheese
1 pound (2 cups) chopped smoked salmon

Preheat oven to 350°. Combine Parmesan cheese, breadcrumbs, and butter until thoroughly blended, and press mixture into bottom of 9-inch springform pan. Bake 7 minutes.

Heat oil in medium skillet over high heat. Add onions and bell peppers and sauté, stirring and shaking the skillet, for 2 minutes. Stir in salt and pepper, sauté for 1 minute, and remove from the heat. Using an electric mixer, beat the cream cheese with the eggs in a large bowl until very thick and frothy, about 4 minutes. Mix in the cream, Gouda cheese, the sautéed vegetables, and the smoked salmon, and beat until thoroughly incorporated and creamy, for about 2 minutes.

Pour the filling over the crust in the springform pan. Wrap bottom of springform pan in foil and place in 13 x 9" pan filled with hot water that measures $\frac{1}{4}$ of the way up the sides of the springform pan. Bake until firm, about 1 hour and 15 minutes. Allow to cool to room temperature. If you refrigerate the cheesecake before serving, remove from the refrigerator and allow it to come to room temperature for about an hour.

Optional: garnish with garlic chive mayonnaise, fresh dill, and caviar.

Glass Chimney
CARMEL

12901 Old Meridian Street   (317) 844-0921

Open Monday–Thursday 6–10 P.M.,
Friday–Saturday 6–11 P.M.

In 1976, a young Austrian-born chef named Dieter Puska and his wife, Hermie, opened a cozy nook of a restaurant next to a laundromat in a nondescript shopping strip off the corner of Main Street and Old Meridian in Carmel, immediately east of U.S. 31 North. It was Puska's first venture as owner and chef, after apprenticing at such celebrated kitchens as the Maisonette in Cincinnati and Chanteclair and the late King Cole in Indianapolis. The Glass Chimney drew almost immediate acclaim. The clientele, dazzled by the quality and innovation of Puska's European-influenced cuisine, were stunned but grateful that such a creative bistro had found its way into the aggressively grilled meat-and-potato sentiments of the 1970s Hoosier dining landscape.

They reveled in his 20-item appetizer repertoire, which included Strasbourg goose liver pâté, chopped lamb in rolled cabbage leaf, and Beluga caviar; main entrées such as roast duck in lingonberry sauce; pepper-seared, cognac-flamed steak au poivre; his cotelettes d' agneau boulangère (a casserole of lamb chops baked over onions and sliced potatoes); and such rousing desserts as crêpes Suzette, bananas Foster, and cherries jubilee (for two).

Late in 1979, the Puskas were able to gain some breathing and elbow room when a much larger restaurant facility became available just around the corner on Old Meridian Street. The Glass Chimney took on a classier look, with seating for 150. But, concluding that his new digs were too big to do full justice to his refined menu, Puska decided to turn over roughly a third of the space to create a more casual, lower-priced companion to be called Deeter's Nasch and Nip, with chef Dieter deliberately misspelling his name so as not to give the impression that it was designed to cater to sanctimonious *dieters*. For Puska has made very clear in both forums that, in his kitchens, food is a celebration and art form, not an exercise in sacrifice and self-denial.

The Glass Chimney has two quietly elegant dining rooms suitable for special occasions. His menu speaks English, French, and Dieter's native tongue, Austrian, fluently, with delicate cream, wine, and cognac sauces over beef, veal, lamb, and fresh fish à la Française; lightly breaded veal, pork, or trout for a buttery pan sauté with a touch of Austria; and in recent years, embracing the unsung American regional dining experience with Black Angus beef, Provini veal chops, venison, and rib-eyes in a glaze of honey and Jack Daniels.

The 46-seat Deeter's Nasch and Nip provides more muscular fare in a more festive, chattier atmosphere: steaks, roast chicken and duckling, veal schnitzels, walleye and trout, and—for true believers—veal liver sautéed with onions and bacon. The decor in Deeter's underwent a sleeker, more contemporary facelift from the original Austrian-mountain lodge ambience, complete with a large tank filled with trout. Also fine-tuned is the bar area, where patrons can settle in for the evening, immersing themselves in the stunning appetizer menu featuring pan- and pepper-seared rare ahi tuna in a honey soy glaze, Cajun-fried chicken livers, artichokes stuffed with prosciutto and goat cheese, and whatever culinary whims Dieter and his kitchen staff are entertaining that afternoon.

As you make your way around the Hoosier state, you may find many of Dieter Puska's triumphs making guest appearances in small fine-dining bistros that popped up during the '90s. In much the same way that college basketball coaches have been spawned from the players and assistants who survived and benefitted from Bobby Knight's hard-driving, demanding program at Indiana University, the kitchens of the Glass Chimney have produced some of the best young chefs in Indiana. These are now embarking on successful culinary ventures of their own, having learned their art from chef Dieter, who set the standard for fine dining in Indiana.

WIENER KALBSEINMACH SUPPE (Viennese-style Veal Soup)

4–6 tablespoons clarified butter	bay leaf
2 onions, diced	2½ gallons chicken stock
4 carrots, diced	salt and pepper to taste
4 ribs celery, diced	fresh parsley
2 pounds veal stew meat,	fresh thyme
in ½ inch squares	8 eggs

Heat a 5-gallon soup pot, adding butter. Add onion, carrots, and celery, and sauté lightly for 3 minutes. Add the veal, bay leaf, and chicken stock, and season with salt and pepper to taste. Simmer for 40–45 minutes, or until veal is tender. At this point, add parsley and thyme and adjust the seasonings.

Off heat, whisk in eggs. Bring the soup back to a boil. Consistency may be adjusted by adding a small amount of roux. (This makes approximately 20–25 servings.)

CRÈME CARAMEL (for 8 3-ounce custards)

2 cups milk	2 cups sugar
1 cup heavy cream	7 eggs
1 vanilla bean	2 egg yolks

In a small saucepan, mix $\frac{1}{2}$ of the sugar with 3 ounces of water, and allow the sugar to turn a rich caramel color. Carefully pour caramelized sugar into 3-ounce dishes.

In a larger pot, heat milk, cream, vanilla bean, and sugar.

In a mixing bowl, beat eggs and egg yolks. Once the cream and milk have come to a simmer, slowly temper the milk and cream mixture into the bowl with the eggs. Strain this custard through a strainer.

Then fill each dish with 3 ounces custard. Bake in a water bath in an oven preheated to 325° for 50–60 minutes.

Gray Brothers Cafeteria
MOORESVILLE

State Roads 67 and 267   (765) 831-3345

Hours: 11 A.M.–9 P.M. Monday–Sunday

In 1944, Forrest Gray opened a modest short order, country-cooking operation in downtown Mooresville, calling it Gray's Restaurant. It was his two sons, Lawrence and Kenny, a few years later who turned it into the cafeteria icon it is today, where people come to—as they say in these parts—"load up and eat" on fried chicken, carved roast beef, mashed potatoes, green beans with bacon, chicken and noodles, chicken livers, baked fish, lasagna, macaroni and cheese, fresh rolls, and pies.

Business in downtown Mooresville was humming nicely for Gray Brothers Cafeteria when it occurred to the brothers Gray they might attract a few more customers if they moved out onto the main highway east of town. In 1969, they opened a new, larger cafeteria out all by its lonesome on SR 67. Soon folks from Indianapolis and surrounding locales were finding excuses to travel up and down SR 67 for some major pit stop nourishment at Gray Brothers. Many made a special point of popping in on Sundays after church, lined up into the parking lot and adjoining fields at peak hours, for the food reminded them of the spread Grandma used to lay on of a Sunday afternoon—at least until Grandma started coaching girls' soccer.

In the early going, Lawrence and Kenny were surprised by the onslaught and inadequately staffed to handle it. Neither would permit himself a day off. Any free time seemed to be spent expanding and redecorating the restaurant, four times in all, to produce its current seating capacity of 550 and spacious country-charm decor. In the '90s, Lawrence and Kenny were able glide into quality control consultant status between sabbaticals to warmer climes, turning the operations over to their children: Merrill, Jeff, and Lynna from the Lawrence wing; Michael, Chris, and Theresa from the Kenny branch. There will always be Grays on the premises to guide the staff of 135, which each week fries up 5,000 pounds of chicken, carves 2,000 pounds of roast beef, and bakes 3,000 fruit and cream pies, most of which will be poised at the very beginning of the cafeteria line, at the point of least resistance.

Gray's signature pie is the strawberry, which is also the top seller at the carry-out store they added to the restaurant in the late '80s. Their staff had to be resuscitated when on the first Thanksgiving eve that the carry-out was open, Gray Brothers sold 1,800 strawberry pies for home consumption, in addition to the 1,200 strawberry pies they were making for those dropping in for Thanksgiving dinner. That's a lot of strawberries that have to be rustled up wherever they're in season for a restaurant that only closes on Christmas Day!

It explains why Gray Brothers has clocked in over half a century as one of Indiana's highest volume eateries, being there every day to deliver what Hoosiers and their friends and relatives from out of town always have a taste for.

Hollyhock Hill
INDIANAPOLIS

8110 N. College Ave.   (317) 251-2294

Open Tuesday–Saturday 5–8 P.M., Sunday 12–7:30 P.M.

Hollyhock Hill is named after the colorful flowers that grace the grounds of this family-dining icon in the 8100-block of North College Avenue in Indianapolis. The hollyhocks were presumably in place when it began life as the Country Cottage under the proprietorship of V. D. Vincent and his wife, Elizabeth. Their cozy 40-seat café was most definitely out in the country, and duly marketed that way, as the Vincents ran ads urging the Indianapolis business community and its residents to hold business meetings and social gatherings at their bucolic cottage to "get away once in awhile from city hustle, noise, and din. Get away from the mine run of club and hotel service. Relax on a leisurely drive to this beautiful part of our 'No Mean City.'"

"No Mean City," as a city historian referred to it, eventually reached Hollyhock Hill in the form of pleasant neighborhoods, but allowed the restaurant to maintain its rural charms. The death of Mr. Vincent in the '40s, and the gas rationing that sharply restricted deliveries of food, supplies, and ice to the restaurant, prompted Mrs. Vincent to close Country Cottage during the war. A local attorney named "Buzz" Watson bought the restaurant shortly afterwards and ran it until 1947, when he sold to Hubert and Marie Kelso.

Hubert Kelso, a native of Rushville, was fresh from the Army and looking for a business he and his wife could superintend. While not well versed in the culinary arts, Kelso did inherit a quintet of ladies in the kitchen who were—operating from recipes in their head, not on paper—true to the "little bit of this, just a pinch of that" school of country cooking. The Kelsos set about transforming the restaurant, changing the name to Hollyhock Hill in honor of the flowers and making skillet-fried chicken, coated in flour and fried in lard, their showcase menu item, offered family style, with tureens of whipped potatoes, chicken gravy, vegetables, fresh-baked bread, and ice cream sundaes for the finale.

Fried shrimp and steaks also achieved star billing on the menu, and all meals featured their signature sweet-and-sour salad with pickled beets. The restaurant's rousing success resulted in extensive remodeling and expansion to two dining rooms with seating for 130, particularly attuned to large family gatherings enamored of its spirit of "Sunday dinner at Grandmas," and where Grandma insisted the brood gather on her birthday and Mother's Day. Kelso built special cookers and fryers to handle up to 200 pieces of chicken at a time.

This intergenerational link has allowed Hollyhock Hill to endure the onslaught of franchise competition. With the Kelsos' formal retirement in 1992, Jay and Barbara Snyder assumed the mantle of ownership. Unlike 1947, when Hubert and Marie took over, Jay and Barbara did not have to pause and reflect on their first days as owner. It was just another day at the office, for Jay has been with Hollyhock Hill since he was a 15-year-old freshman at Broad Ripple High School in the early '60s—mowing lawns, washing windows, busing tables, working his way up to running the kitchen and managing the restaurant. Barbara worked as a waitress and hostess. Now as owners, they are as much married to Hollyhock as they are to each other, with 16-hour days and the Kelsos living next door available for consulting and quality control.

CINDY'S SALAD (serves 6 to 8)

1 head romaine lettuce
1 cup shredded mozzarella
1 cup croutons
$\frac{1}{2}$ cup slivered almonds, toasted

2 chopped green onions
1 small can mandarin oranges, drained
2 chopped hard-boiled eggs

Toss all of the ingredients in bowl, and serve with Hollyhock Hill Head Lettuce Dressing, available at restaurant.

CINDY'S COLE SLAW

1 head cabbage

Hollyhock Hill Head Lettuce Dressing

Finely shred the cabbage. Mix in dressing.

Note: Hollyhock Hill Head Lettuce Dressing is a sweet sugar and vinegar–based oil salad dressing. Another vinaigrette-type dressing could be substituted.

Iaria's Italian Restaurant
INDIANAPOLIS

317 S. College Avenue   (317) 638-7706/632-0667

Open Tuesday–Thursday 11 A.M.–9:30 P.M.,
Friday 11 A.M.–10:30 P.M., Saturday 3–10:30 P.M.

The early 1930s saw two Italian-accented eateries open just a block from each other on South College Avenue. Both still prosper, one as a continuing family operation (Iaria's), the other born again (Milano Inn; see below).

Pete and Antoinette Iaria opened their Italian restaurant in a narrow two-story building on the southern edge of downtown Indianapolis in 1933, securing what is believed to be the first liquor license issued by the city following the repeal of Prohibition. The Iarias had come to Indianapolis with their eight children in 1911 from Italy by way of West Virginia and had been involved in the retail food business at Indianapolis' downtown City Market and the Lockerbie neighborhood on the near eastside.

They came to the restaurant business armed with Antoinette's formidable tomato sauce recipe, liberally applied to hearty portions of spaghetti, ravioli, lasagna, capellini, mostaccioli, chicken cacciatore, veal Parmesan, meatballs, and pizzas. Antoinette displayed her talents for direct marketing by going to the nearby G & J Rubber Company plant and passing out free samples of food to its employees. Iaria's was soon on firm footing as a neighborhood restaurant.

Pete and Antoinette brought sons Matthew and Rocco into the business in the '50s. The restaurant had been situated in an area plagued by periodic spring flooding; at this time the family built the current forum, divided into dining room and bar, on higher ground nearby for their hearty, reliable takes on traditional southern Italian fare. Matthew and Rocco's no-nonsense approach toward the preparation and quality of their cuisine and toward the proper behavior of bar patrons have kept Iaria's reputation as a neighborhood restaurant intact.

It was with a somewhat wary eye that Matthew greeted his son Nick's renovation plans when Nick took over the restaurant in the '70s. The Italian and Irish neighborhoods Iaria's had served were now virtually a memory, and Nick figured that the restaurant needed a facelift to attract new diners from the downtown office buildings and throughout the city. He also added some contemporary touches to the menu, such as fettuccine Alfredo; eggplant, veal, and chicken Parmesan; and veal and chicken piccata. Thus the usual generational arguments over fixing things that ain't broke and spending money to make money ensued, but Nick won out, and earned his dad's very grudging respect when Iaria's continued to endure and endear.

Matt Iaria died in 1999 at the age of 90, secure that his parents' dining legacy was in good hands with Nick and his wife, Kathleen, and his mother's tomato sauce percolating in the basement for six hours each day prior to opening. And as at St. Elmo Steak House, the hallway between the dining room and bar is adorned with signed photos of assorted entertainers and athletes who came and come to Iaria's for a major carbohydrate injection while in town. Iaria's has been a particular favorite for that trencherman species known as basketball coaches with names like Knight, Bird, Pitino, Carlisimo, and Fretello, as well as one regular from the auto racing fraternity named Mario Andretti, who should know a little something about how Italian cuisine should be prepared.

FETTUCCINE ALFREDO (approximately 5 servings)

1 quart heavy whipping cream
2½ cups Parmesan cheese, grated
1 cup whipped butter
¼ tablespoon chopped garlic

salt and pepper to taste
dash nutmeg
2 pounds fettuccine noodles, cooked and drained
parsley, minced

Place butter, garlic, and cream in a skillet or saucepan, and simmer on medium heat until it starts to boil. Add Parmesan cheese and stir constantly with a whisk to prevent sticking or clumping until sauce is of even consistency and has thickened to desired point. *Note:* The longer it cooks, the thicker the sauce will be.

Add cooked fettuccine to the sauce and toss until all noodles are coated with sauce. Plate the coated noodles and add a dash of nutmeg and parsley to each plate for garnish.

CANNOLI FILLING (for approximately 12–16 cannoli)

2 pounds ricotta cheese	1½ cups sifted powdered sugar
4 ounces orange juice	3 ounces chocolate chips
1 ounce Triple Sec	⅛ teaspoon vanilla
⅛ teaspoon cinnamon	cannoli shells

Combine all the ingredients into a mixing bowl and stir until thick and creamy. Spoon the mix into a pastry bag and squeeze into cannoli shells. Garnish with powdered sugar, chocolate syrup, and/or cherries if desired.

Iron Skillet
INDIANAPOLIS

2489 W. 30th Street   (317) 923-6353

Open Wednesday–Saturday 5:30–8:30 P.M.,
Sunday noon–7:30 P.M.

The Iron Skillet stands rather majestically atop a hill overlooking the public Riverside Golf Course off West 30th Street and Cold Spring Road in Indianapolis, in a two-story white house that once served as a clubhouse when the course was part of the Highland Country Club. Originally built around 1880 as the home of August Wacker, a German-born entrepreneur and civic leader, it was used during World War II by military forces stationed at the nearby naval armory.

In the '50s the golf course became the property of the city of Indianapolis, which wasn't sure precisely what to do with that nice house on the hill. Enter Hubert Kelso, owner of Hollyhock Hill restaurant, and food distributor Jim McFarling, who supplied Hollyhock with its celebrated chicken. Both convinced the city to lease the building for a family restaurant in the culinary image and likeness of Hollyhock Hill.

And who better to operate it for them than Hubert's kid brother, Charles Kelso, and his wife Patricia, under the banner of McFarling Foods? Charles proceeded to learn the family restaurant secrets during a training stint at Hollyhock Hill. Then he and Patricia purchased the restaurant in 1956, dubbing it the Iron Skillet in tribute to the optimal kitchen utensil for fried chicken, and immersing themselves in the winning Hollyhock formula: family-style skillet-fried chicken, along with steaks, fried shrimp, and walleyed pike, in a charming setting of white tablecloths, candlelight, fresh flowers, and latticework in three dining rooms. So attentive was Kelso that customers making phone reservations would be asked whether they would be having chicken, and if so, what their preferences were regarding white and/or dark meat. Soon the old Wacker home was humming with enthusiastic diners.

The restaurant became a reliable venue for wedding rehearsal dinners and receptions, reunions, club meetings, and Christmas gatherings and has been a popular pit stop in the month of May for those involved in or observing the preparations for the Greatest Spectacle in Racing at a track just south of there. Customers frequently inquired where the Kelsos obtained their copper tea kettles, glassware, candelabra, and other accouterments, so they put a gift shop on the second floor.

In 1996, the Kelsos sold the restaurant to its manager Ronald Turk, but Charles is still there, providing expertise and quality control and asking customers, "How would you like your chicken?"

BROWNIES (for 2 pans)

8 squares unsweetened chocolate	8 eggs
1 cup butter	2 teaspoons vanilla
4 cups white sugar	1 teaspoon salt
1 two-top gravy bowl flour	

Preheat oven to 350°. Melt the chocolate and butter slowly in a small saucepan. Mix the sugar, eggs, vanilla, and salt before adding the flour. After the flour has been added, continue to beat the mix until thoroughly combined. At this point, the butter and chocolate should be added, and mix it all very well. Spray the brownie pans with Vegelene (*note:* Pam can be substituted). Line the bottom of each pan with wax paper. Spray the top of the wax paper with a liberal coat of Vegelene as well. Divide the brownie mix evenly between the two pans. Bake for 25 minutes turning the pans once at the 12-minute mark to promote even baking. Meanwhile get two large trays and turn them upside down. Cover each tray with wax paper. After removing the brownies from the oven, cover the pans with the trays. Use the tray to support the brownies while inverting the pan to remove them. Carefully remove the wax paper from the brownies, and immediately cut them into four columns and 12 rows with a bread knife.

PICKLED BEETS

6 #10 cans whole small beets   pickling spices
white vinegar   1 tablespoon salt
5 pounds sugar, plus 5 cups sugar

Place beets in a pot. Cover with white vinegar. Put the sugar on top of the beets and vinegar. Add scant handful of pickling spices and salt. Let all this come to a boil, and then shut off. Place beets in sterilized jars.

Janko's Little Zagreb
BLOOMINGTON

223 W. 6th Street   (812) 332-0694

Open Monday–Thursday 5–9:30 P.M.,
Friday–Saturday 4:30–10 P.M.

Janko's Little Zagreb is the place that instantly comes to mind when Bloomington carnivores get a yen for a little something from the hoof. Slabs of rib-eyes, T-bones, porterhouses, sirloins, and filets have been made available in its well-worn, charmingly weathered, creaky-floored edifice at 6th and Morton streets, a block west of the Square, against the railroad tracks.

The two-story structure was built in 1916 and used first as a feed store, then soon after as a tavern (the Royal Oak) to serve the thirst and entertainment needs of railroad workers. Upstairs rooms were rented out to Pullman porters in need of overnight lodging while working the Chicago to Indianapolis run. Allegedly, they were also used to entertain ladies who made their charms and companionship readily accessible in a part of town that came to be called the Levee, whose free-spirited reputation went unmentioned in Bloomington tourist brochures and Chamber of Commerce presentations.

Inspired by this railroad legacy, Jeffrey Pouch first called the restaurant he opened there in 1972 the Choo-Chew Café. He was soon joined by his brother, John, better known as Janko ("Little John") to his Croatian relatives in his native Hammond. Initially the Choo-Chew stressed the cuisine found in the restaurants of Yugoslavia and Eastern Europe: the stuffed pepper dish called punjene paprike; the provolone-topped eggplant and vegetable triumph called palidzan-sa-sirom; highly spiced meatballs and sausages; and lamb and beef shish kebob.

While those hearty entrées still have a cherished place on the menu, ultimately what earned Bloomington's affection and patronage was the Pouches' steaks. They came from herds of cattle raised on Janko's farm in Spencer and butchered and processed by the Bloomington Packing Company. Janko also raised sheep for Choo-Chew's lamb dishes, and the Pouches developed a strong relationship with Hayes Market, across the street, for fresh meats and produce. As their business increased, it became too much of a chore to raise the cattle and fight off the wild dogs of sweet Owen County who harassed the sheep. So the Pouches let the standard meat suppliers supply their fresh beef and lamb.

In 1979, Jeff Pouch headed west to work for the Hilton hotel chain, and Janko assumed command. He changed the restaurant's name to Little Zagreb, in honor of his Yugoslavian roots, and gave the restaurant a drastic fashion makeover inspired by one Robert Montgomery Knight, whose tenure as Indiana University's resident basketball genius coincided with Little Zagreb's birth and development.

Under Jeff, the restaurant had possessed the dark, Bohemian look of a Greenwich Village basement bistro, where you might expect a beat poetry reading to break out. But Janko, noting the throngs of IU fans flocking to Little Zagreb's on game nights to load up on pre-game protein and carbs, apparently enlisted Coach Knight as his interior decorator, for the restaurant is awash in IU cream and crimson, with red and white checked tablecloths and IU basketball schedule posters of yore adorning the walls of the two dining rooms. In the back room, Janko has a special table with legs four inches higher than the other tables, to accommodate IU's coach and five of his hoops posse.

But whatever you think of the decor, the sound and scent of steaks, lamb, and pork chops sizzling on the grill near the front entrance will lure you into Little Zagreb whether IU is playing that night or not.

LITTLE ZAGREB'S EGGPLANT PROVOLONE

2 large cans cooked tomatoes, drained (approximately 1 pint)

2 large cans tomato sauce, approximately 28 ounces total

4 cloves garlic, peeled, chopped, and crushed

1 stalk celery, chopped into small but not fine pieces

2 large green peppers, chopped in small but not fine pieces

2 large Spanish onions, chopped into small, but not fine pieces

1 bunch parsley, chopped

1 tablespoon black pepper

6 large eggplants peeled and cubed in 1½ inch portions

2 pounds grated provolone cheese

½ cup grated Romano cheese

You will need two large pans.

In Pan #1: Bring tomatoes and tomato sauce to a hard simmer. Add garlic, black pepper, and if desired, salt, and bring back to hard simmer. Add the chopped celery, green peppers, onions, and parsley, and bring back to hard simmer. Simmer over medium heat 10 minutes, and stir while cooking.

Pan #2 (a spaghetti cooker or all-purpose pan): Steam the eggplants until tender, but not mushy, for approximately 15 minutes. Do *not* immerse eggplants in water. Drain eggplants, and put into Pan #1, stirring the contents as you add, and simmering lightly in the sauce for about 5 minutes. Take desired portion out of Pan #1, and top it generously with the grated provolone and Romano cheeses. Bake or microwave until the cheeses melt on top. Serve in a large casserole dish, or an individualized portion container.

LITTLE ZAGREB'S BROCCOLI CHEDDAR SOUP

2 large cans chicken stock (approximately 3 quarts)

1 stalk (head) celery, chopped, but not finely

2 large Spanish onions, chopped, but not finely

6 medium bunches broccoli, sliced, with the flower tops set aside

2 sticks butter

1 bunch parsley, chopped

black pepper to taste

2 tablespoons dry mustard

3 tablespoons leaf oregano

3 cups white sauce (using 4 tablespoons flour and 1 tablespoon black pepper to 1 cup flour. Any lumps in the white sauce should be removed with potato masher or blender)

2 pounds New York sharp cheddar cheese, grated and kept separate

4 cups milk

Base: Bring chicken stock to a boil. Add celery, onions, and broccoli stems to the chicken stock. Bring first to a boil, then to a hard simmer, cooking vegetables for approximately 8 minutes until the broccoli stems start to change color. Add butter, broccoli flower tops, and parsley, and bring to a boil again. Add black pepper, dry mustard, and leaf oregano. Stir in white sauce slowly to desired thickness.

Final product: In cooking over double boiler, use the amount needed per meal. Make sure the base is thoroughly heated and hot. Add grated cheddar cheese and milk to the desired amount per meal.

Janko's Notes: Always use a larger pan than you think you might need.

Recipe makes a large amount of soup base, but I don't guarantee results if it is cut. The base freezes well; frozen in suitable containers, it can be thawed and used as needed. Simply add grated cheese and milk after heating.

Kopper Kettle Inn
MORRISTOWN

State Road 52   (765) 763-6767

Open for lunch and dinner Tuesday–Saturday
11 A.M.–8:30 P.M. (last seating),
Sunday 11:30 A.M.–6:30 P.M. (last seating)

What has set the 75-year-old Kopper Kettle apart from the rest of Indiana's icon restaurants is that through most of its existence it was owned and operated by women. Muriel Vredenberg first established her dream project on State Road 52, as it passes through Morristown in east central Indiana, in a hotel once owned by her great-grandparents, Thornton and Betsy Rogers.

At its birth in the 1830s, this hotel was a stagecoach stop along the dirt road between Indianapolis and Cincinnati. In the late 1840s, the Junction Railroad came through Morristown as part of its 25-mile run from Shelbyville to Knightstown, prompting the building's owners to conclude that it would be more profitably used as a grain elevator. But when the Junction Railroad stopped coming through town in 1858, the building came under the control of Nancy Owens

Davis, who had the inspiration of turning it into a tavern, located on the spot of the Kopper Kettle's current foyer and appropriately dubbed the Old Davis Tavern.

Two year later, Davis sold the watering hole to Thornton and Betsy Rogers, who presided over it for the next 11 years, until Thornton Rogers's death in 1885. Heirs and subsequent owners expanded the building and oversaw its transition from the Old Davis Tavern to the Valley House, a hotel offering what was advertised as "13 well-ventilated rooms."

Meanwhile, the Rogerses' great-granddaughter, Muriel, married Robert Vredenburg, a furniture salesman, and started making a name for herself in Shelbyville, buying old homes, fixing them up with decorator flair, and then reselling them. Her dream was to open a tea room with European panache, and, for sentimental reasons, she had her eye on that little hotel in Morristown that her great-grandparents had once owned. By 1923, she had the down payment and was ready to fulfill the vision.

It was a vision undaunted by the collapse of her marriage and by conventional 1920s assumptions that there was no way for a single woman, let alone a single mother, to be so foolish as to think she could run a hotel and restaurant alone. The confident and focused Muriel Vredenburg knew better, and males of the species with whom she had to deal in the way of salesmen, suppliers, vendors, and customers soon had their skepticism, doubts, and smirks erased.

She started by closing the hotel operation in 1927 to focus on a restaurant that would create the atmosphere of Sunday dinner at Grandma's. Folks from Indiana and Ohio found themselves making the country drive for "pass-the-mashed-potatoes-and-green-beans" family-style dinners, revolving around skillet-fried chicken, steak, and fried shrimp, then loosening their belts for sugar cream and banana cream pies. In her extensive travels out east, Muriel had taken a shine to the look and elegance of copper kettles, and decided not only that her coffee and tea would be served in such vessels, but that her dream restaurant would bear the name Kopper Kettle—spelled with K's, over the protests of her young daughter, Millie, to make it catchier.

Muriel's dining rooms quickly became as sumptuous as her

meals, decorated with antiques and art pieces and glittering chandeliers, even a grand piano or two, each table with a style and personality all its own, each chair an antique. Patrons found themselves walking carefully for fear of brushing up against and breaking something valuable. Indeed, still on display are a select few Chinese *objets d'art* brought back in the '20s by Muriel's twin missionary aunts, Muriel and Miriam, who answered Evangelist Billy Sunday's call to spread the gospel in China only to be forced to return home on the heels of the Boxer Rebellion. After that, they ran successful gift shops specializing in Oriental artifacts.

Upon Muriel's death in 1972 at age 84, her daughter, Mildred "Millie" Taylor assumed command, with the help of her husband, Lyle, eventually bringing her eldest daughter, Lisa, into the business as manager. Millie expanded the dining facilities in a series of fetching remodelings, resulting in an attractive outdoor courtyard.

After all these years, the country menu remains untouched at virtual customer insistence, for the Kopper Kettle has long been a favorite for family gatherings. Folks book a year ahead for Easter, Mother's Day, Thanksgiving, and Christmas Eve celebrations, not to mention the annual holiday get-togethers of friends and office bonding in December. And through the decades, the Kopper Kettle guest register has taken note of such luminaries as Henry Ford, Herbert Hoover, Charles Lindbergh, and assorted Hoosier governors and heads of state.

Millie's desire to retire, and Lisa's decision to move to Florida, prompted Millie in 1997 to develop a partnership with Leigh and Kristi Langkabel to lead the Kopper Kettle into the 21st century while never forgetting what got them so prosperously through the 20th.

COUNTRY GREEN BEANS

1 6-pound can cut green beans including liquid, or 3 pounds fresh green beans, cleaned and snapped	$^1/_4$ large onion 1 teaspoon salt 2 tablespoons brown sugar $^1/_2$ cup diced jowl bacon

Place beans with liquid in a large kettle. Add onion, salt, brown sugar, and jowl bacon. Bring the beans to a boil, then reduce heat

and simmer, covered, 4–6 hours, stirring occasionally. Remove onion and discard before serving. Enjoy.

GOLDEN PAN-FRIED COUNTRY CHICKEN

Flour, enough to cover chicken
Salt and pepper to taste
Lard, enough to cover one inch
 of the skillet

½ cup sugar, ½ cup salt, and
1 gallon water to create the
honey dip for the chicken

In the skillet, put one inch lard to cover skillet, after pre-heating to
350°. Wash the chicken in 120° water for 3 minutes. This will heat
chicken, to insure the meat will be cooked all the way through. Place
chicken in honey dip (made of ½ cup each sugar and salt and 1
gallon water) so the flour sticks to the chicken. Bread the chicken in
the flour, salting and peppering to taste. Place chicken in frying pan
with best side down. Cover the frying pan and cook approximately
15 minutes on medium flame.

Uncover chicken and turn over when bottom side is golden
brown.

Leaving lid off, cook approximately 5–10 minutes until the
opposite side is golden brown. Enjoy.

Log Inn
WARRENTON

Old State Road (one mile east of U.S. 41)   (812) 867-3216

Open for dinner Tuesday–Saturday 4–10 P.M.

In 1963 John Rettig discovered that his restaurant in the tiny hamlet
of Warrenton, a mile east of U.S. 41, 12 miles north of Evansville,
was the oldest restaurant in Indiana. Some weatherbeaten boards
had come loose after a storm to reveal huge yellow poplar logs
underneath, and, ultimately, some rich history and lore.

After dogged research in musty court records, Rettig discovered
that the Log Inn had been built in 1825 as a stagecoach stop along
the Old State Road between Evansville and Terre Haute, originally
an Indian trail. It also functioned as a trading post. The town of

Warrenton grew up around it, founded in 1840 and named after Revolutionary War hero General Joseph Warren. Among the Log Inn's early owners was an early entrepreneur named Henry Haub, who founded the nearby community of Haubstadt in 1855.

A German-Jewish entrepreneur named Meier Heiman took over in late 1852, and 15 years later decided this stagecoach stop needed to go to the next level. He, his brothers Leon, Jacob, and J.L., and the father-and-son carpentry team of Heinrich and Henry Loewencamp added on to the log section, creating something of a frontier convenience center with all manner of groceries, goods, and services, including a tavern, a dance hall upstairs, and a separate barn for a lucrative sideline—mule sales and service. The log section became family living quarters. During the remodeling process, the logs were covered with hand-split hickory laths in the interest of what was then considered a sleeker, trendier look.

The tavern attracted a lively clientele, including construction workers drawn from a stretch of the Erie Canal seven miles away. Payday was a spirited occasion during this period. Whiskey went down in copious amounts, and freelance brawling soon commenced. The Heiman brothers took the money, but not the guff, as they skillfully guided the combatants from the premises.

After 43 years of stewardship, the Heimans sold out to Joe Reinhart in 1895 in order to go into the mule barn business in Evansville. Among Reinhart's major orders of business was to reinforce the dance floor above the bar lest some night the dancers should come cascading down on the barflies below. Subsequent owners from the George Memmer family finally built a ground-level dance floor in back of the building, where it currently functions primarily as a banquet and meeting facility, but one able to withstand any dance sensation one cares to inflict on it.

John and Victoria Rettig bought the establishment in May of 1947, with the hidden log section still serving as family living quarters. With Rettig involved in his tool-and-die business, Victoria and her father, Charlie Wassmer, ran the restaurant, heretofore better known for its fried pork brain sandwiches. Victoria elevated the cuisine to a classic and comforting country menu, with fried chicken, roast beef, ham, hot German potato salad, mashed potatoes and gravy, and an extensive pie repertoire.

The 1963 unearthing of those magnificent logs inspired Rettig to restore the original log section and make it the crown jewel of the Log Inn's dining rooms. The centerpiece is an 1850s-vintage pot-bellied stove that once served the heating needs of the Inglefield train depot. On one of the walls is a picture of Irish-born Thomas Conner, who drove stagecoaches in and out of the Warrenton stop in the late 1830s.

Given a special place of honor in this room is a portrait of the Log Inn's most prominent customer, Abraham Lincoln, who supposedly once enjoyed a dish of peaches and cream as he awaited the stagecoach home in November 1844. After four terms in the Illinois House, Mr. Lincoln was between political gigs, in private law practice in Springfield, Illinois, but was soon to embark on a successful campaign for Congress. 16 years later, he was elected president. As Log Inn patrons have often remarked since then, "Who knew?"

It is fitting that another aspect of Log Inn's legend and lore is that the cellar beneath the building is believed to have been used as a hiding place for runaway slaves as part of the Underground Railroad system.

Rita Elpers, the current owner, is well versed in all aspects of the Log Inn, having literally grown up within its walls as the daughter of John and Victoria Rettig. She and her husband, Gene, took over in 1978, utilizing Gene's professional carpentry skills to expand regular seating to 475, with an additional dining room in the rustic spirit of the original, from logs obtained from an old log church. Their three children are now also active in the business. The reputation of the Log Inn's country menu and its historic legacy make it one of southern Indiana's most popular weekend dining destinations. For the record, that menu no longer lists peaches and cream, but I suspect that if a certain prized customer ordered it, the Elpers would see he got it . . . and perhaps even on the house.

LOG INN CHEESECAKE

Crust:

1½ sticks margarine, melted	1 cup sugar
3 cups graham cracker crumbs	

Mix graham cracker crumbs and sugar together. Stir in melted margarine. Reserving a cup of this mixture for the topping, place remainder in a 9x13" pan. Press together to make a crust.

Filling:

1 cup boiling water
1 3-ounce package lemon Jello
1 cup crushed ice
12 ounces cream cheese, softened

1 cup sugar
1 teaspoon vanilla
1 tall can Milnot

Pour Jello into boiling water. Stir until dissolved. Add ice, and stir until it is melted. Set in the freezer until it jells. Beat cream cheese, sugar, and vanilla until creamy. Add Jello mixture. Set in the freezer for 2 hours. Beat Milnot until it is in soft peaks. Fold into Jello mixture. Pour into graham cracker crust. Sprinkle remainder of graham cracker crumbs over the top. Chill several hours.

FRESH STRAWBERRY PIE

1 cup sugar
1½ cup water
2 tablespoons cornstarch

1 3-ounce package strawberry Jello
1 quart fresh strawberries,
   washed and sliced

Mix together sugar, water, and cornstarch. Cook until texture is thick, stirring constantly. Add Jello. Add strawberries. Pour into a baked pie shell. Refrigerate until set (approximately 3 hours).

Maple Corner Restaurant
COVINGTON

1126 Liberty Street State Road 136   (765) 793-2224

Open Monday–Thursday 4:30–9 P.M., Friday–Saturday
4:30–10 P.M., Sunday 11:30 A.M.–8:30 P.M.

When Sarah Young opened the Maple Corner Restaurant in 1931 in Covington in west central Indiana, she basically had travelers in mind—those wandering through town on State Road 136. It was the classic roadhouse, the walls decorated with the heads of ill-fated animals and large fish on plaques, the menu bragging of fried catfish suppers and cold beer, accessorized by a gas station, small cabins for overnight stays, and several maple trees, which inspired the restaurant's bucolic name.

Subsequent owners John and Clara Belinsky, Tom Ware, Millard and Rosalie Allen, and Rose Martin maintained the cozy, rustic charm and fried catfish nutritional program over the next 42 years. Current owners Jim and Jean Cunningham bought the restaurant in July 1973, on the occasion of their second wedding anniversary, and soon decided it was time for the Maple Corner restaurant to blossom.

Jim Cunningham had grown up on a farm in nearby Illinois, and his family frequently crossed over the state line to dine on catfish at Maple Corner. Since then he had picked up a few skills in carpentry and remodeling. His wife was handy, too. They commenced in 1975 to expand the restaurant, and to expand it some more in 1978, and some more in 1987, and again, once and for all, in 1989. At one point, portable classrooms obtained from Attica High School were used for these expansion projects. When the Cunninghams were done, their 60-seat, two-room roadhouse had mushroomed into nine dining rooms on two levels, capable of serving 600 of the Cunninghams' closest friends, their families, and all the organizations they are members of. Even the Tiffany-style lamps that adorn the rooms were crafted by Jim and Jean.

While the fried catfish still has a cherished spot on the menu, the Cunninghams installed a grill fueled by hickory and sassafras wood to do justice to their line of filets, rib-eyes, porterhouses, one-pound pork chops, marinated chicken breasts, and fresh seafood. The deep fryer accommodates catfish, shrimp, and orange roughy, with an array of combination dinners featuring several permutations on the surf-and-turf concept that are particularly popular among the devoutly eclectic and the chronically indecisive. The white and rye breads that accompany each meal come from Maple Corner's own bakery, as do the baked onion and sweet potato, cheesecake, and apple pies. The recipe for the deep-fried Polish potato dish, pierogi, is courtesy of Jean's mother.

The Cunninghams' various expansion projects have proved to be fully justified. The restaurant draws customers from throughout central Indiana and Illinois, and just about anyone who is passing through or in the neighborhood who is anxious to get off the road and relax with a hearty dinner. It helps explain how a community like Covington, with a population of only 2,000-plus, can support two such major Indiana restaurants as Maple Corner and the Beef House, capable between them of serving over 1,200 on a given night.

COUNTRY APPLE PIE (for 1 medium pie)

9 apples, peeled, cored, and sliced	2 tablespoons flour
1 cup sugar	1½ teaspoons cinnamon

Toss together to mix. Put in 9" deep-dish pie plate lined with crust.

Topping:

½ cup brown sugar	4 ounces butter
1 cup flour	½ cup pecans, chopped

Blend together and put on top of the pie. Bake at 325° for 15–20 minutes. Lower heat to 250° for 50 minutes. Serve warm with slice of cheddar cheese cut in the shape of a maple leaf.

MAPLE CORNER MARGARITAS (for 1 quart)

1½ ounces fresh-squeezed lemon juice	1½ cups tequila
4½ ounces fresh-squeezed lime juice	1½ cups Triple Sec

Mix and pour over ice into salt-rimmed glasses and serve with a wedge of lime; or freeze in blender with a cup of ice.

Milano Inn
INDIANAPOLIS

231 S. College Avenue   (317) 264-3585

Open Monday–Wednesday 11 A.M.–10 P.M., Thursday 11 A.M.–11 P.M., Friday–Saturday 11 A.M.–12 midnight, Sunday 4–9 P.M.

The Milano Inn opened in 1934, one year after and a block north of Iaria's (see above), with Mary and Joe Modaffari taking over a sturdy late 19th century brick building in the 200 block of South College Avenue for well received renditions of spaghetti and meatballs, spaghetti with clam sauce, ravioli, manicotti, mostaccioli, and pizza with assorted toppings.

A conversation piece at the Milano Inn has been the dazzling mural that courses around all four walls of the main dining room, telling the story of the Allied liberation of Italy in World War II. It was created in 1947 at the behest of the Modaffari family by Sergeant Donald Peters, who upon mustering out of the military became a student at the Herron School of Art in Indianapolis. The Modaffaris were admirers of Peters's art, and they commissioned him to paint a mural capturing a moment in their homeland that was near and dear to their hearts and legacy. In exchange, Peters received free room and board for the summer in one of the apartments above the restaurant. In vivid colors, images, and detail, Peters saw to it that each scene in the mural had a riveting story to tell.

The Milano Inn breezed along for over four decades as one of the city's most revered neighborhood Italian restaurants until the passing of Joe and Mary in the late '70s. Other family members tried to keep it going, but by 1980 it appeared to be doomed. Leo LaGrotte, who owned a neighboring railroad equipment salvage business, bought the building with an eye toward tearing it down for expanded parking space.

However, grizzled Milano regulars convinced LaGrotte that with some judicious renovation and an accomplished chef, keeping the Milano Inn alive could be a wise culinary investment. LaGrotte laid on extensive remodeling in 1983, giving the main dining rooms sleek elegance, adding a solarium, and replacing the old apartments upstairs with banquet and party rooms. He even recruited local artist Greg Hughes to paint a large mural on one of the upstairs walls, learning only later that Mr. Hughes is a cousin of Donald Peters.

But Leo LaGrotte's most inspired move was to recruit veteran chef Vickie Dragoo, who took on the challenge with a boxful of recipes designed to bring northern Italian influences to the Milano Inn. Very quickly the luster of the Modafarri years was restored by the LaGrotte/Dragoo partnership, as diners luxuriated in Vickie's exceptionally rich fettuccine Alfredo; her five-layer lasagna timballo; stuffed veal and chicken dishes; shrimp parmigiana and shrimp linguine; and sautéed chicken strips and vegetables in raspberry cream sauce. The Modiffaris' southern-style staples of lasagna, ravioli, and pizza were also given new life.

Mrs. Dragoo passed away in 1997, but her legacy lives on in the menu, and, under the guidance of Leo's daughters, Tina and Gina, the Milano Inn is fully prospering after its near-death experience.

FARFALLE WITH SAUSAGE AND LEEKS

1 raw sausage link, skinned and broken into 6 or 7 pieces
2 teaspoons butter
1 teaspoon chopped garlic
3 ounces sliced leeks
6 ounces chicken stock
6–8 ounces farfalle (bowtie pasta), cooked and drained
1 ounce grated Parmesan cheese
2 tablespoons butter
1 ounce peas

Place 2 teaspoons butter, sausage, garlic, and leeks in sauté pan. Cook in oven at medium to high heat until sausage is almost cooked. Add the chicken stock and peas. Cook until peas are heated through. Add heated bowtie pasta and Parmesan cheese.

To finish, stir in the 2 tablespoons butter and toss until melted. Place on a plate and garnish with Parmesan cheese.

CHICKEN PICCATA

2 boneless chicken breasts (4 ounces each)
2 ounces clarified butter
$\frac{1}{2}$ teaspoon chopped garlic
3 ounces white wine
1 ounce fresh lemon juice
2 lemon slices
1 tablespoon capers
2 ounces unsalted butter
salt and pepper

Pound chicken to uniform thickness and season with salt and pepper. Place skillet over heat and add clarified butter, heating until just before the smoking point. In the meantime, dredge chicken in flour and shake off excess. Place chicken in skillet and cook on first side for 5–6 minutes. Turn over and finish cooking for another 4–5 minutes. Remove chicken from skillet and add garlic, wine, and lemon juice. Get up all little bits stuck to bottom of pan. Next add capers and two lemon slices. Finish sauce by swirling in butter and seasoning with salt and pepper. Return chicken to skillet to heat, then remove to serving plate and pour sauce over top. Serve with side of spaghetti with tomato sauce.

Nashville House
NASHVILLE

Main and Van Buren Streets   (812) 988-4554

Open Sunday–Monday, Wednesday–Thursday
11:30 A.M.–8 P.M., Friday–Saturday 11:30 A.M.-9 P.M.

The Nashville House has long served as the centerpiece of the rustic
tourist mecca that is Nashville, Indiana, offering weary visitors a
respite from a long day of traversing its network of fetching shops
brimming with knickknacks, bric-a-brac, candles, art works, and
items that come under the heading of "stuff." It is the place Brown
County *turistas,* especially the 25,000 who flock there in October to
watch the leaves do their dazzling, color-cavalcaded death dance,
ultimately gather to partake of fried chicken, baked ham and fried
ham steak, roast turkey, ribs, pecan pie, fruit cobblers, and of course
the addictive fried biscuits and baked apple butter.

The Nashville House traces its origins to 1859. As a two-and-a-
half-story hotel, it first catered to loggers toiling in the area's lively
timber trade prior to the Civil War. In the 1920s, it provided comfort to the many artists from the Chicago area and beyond who were
seeking to capture Brown County's forested splendor on canvas.
Nashville became a prominent artist's colony, under the wary, skeptical eyes of the locals.

In 1927, Andrew Jackson Rogers left his Bloomington automobile business and went into partnership with Nashville attorney
Fred Bates Johnson and artist Dale Bessire to buy the hotel and surrounding property, establishing, among other businesses, a thriving
orchard. The trio eventually dissolved their partnership with Johnson assuming control of much prime downtown Nashville real estate, Bessire presiding over the orchard between paintings, and Rogers taking on the hotel with its 13 rooms and popular restaurant.

Fire destroyed the hotel in 1943, but Rogers built a new brick
and poplar wood structure four years later, opting for a restaurant
and country store without lodging. The restaurant put its stress on
fried chicken, fried biscuits, and apple butter. The biscuits were
developed from an old English muffin recipe Rogers came upon.
The baked apple butter used to be made from fresh apples, mixed
with cinnamon and sugar. Now commercial apple sauce is used for

better consistency and expediency. The Old Country Store, located in what was once the lobby of the old hotel, has cast iron and stone cookware, kitchen gadgets, and such sweet somethings to remember them by as home-baked breads, candy, fudge, cookies, and hickory-smoked meats.

Upon Jack Rogers's death in 1959, his son Andy took over the Nashville House and, in subsequent years, much else of significance in developing Nashville as Indiana's premier tourist destination. Now tourists haunt the place from spring through the Christmas holidays, thanks to the mushrooming of shops and restaurants, and most notably hotels like the Seasons and the Brown County Inn, which attract business and academic clientele for meetings, conferences, and symposiums. In seeking to merge Nashville's bucolic allure with commercial appeal, Rogers chronically finds himself the focal point of debates between shopkeepers seeking ever more tourists and native Brown Countians who fear their cherished homeland is losing its quaintness and charm to the demands of the cash register.

All admit that October does wonders for Brown County's economy, especially since industry does not, and it certainly brightens the ledgers of the Nashville House's 110-seat dining room. October days may see as many as 900 customers, many patiently waiting for two or more hours to break biscuits and dip them in apple butter amid poplar-beamed walls and cozy fireplaces, carefully balancing the past and the present.

NASHVILLE HOUSE FRIED BISCUITS

1 quart milk
$\frac{1}{4}$ cup sugar
$2\frac{2}{3}$ package dry yeast, or $\frac{1}{6}$ cup yeast

$\frac{1}{2}$ cup lard or shortening
6 teaspoons salt
7–9 cups flour

Add yeast to warm water. Add other ingredients and let the dough rise. Work into biscuits and drop into hot fat.

NASHVILLE HOUSE COLE SLAW

Mix together shredded cabbage, onion, salt, pepper, mayonnaise, and packaged herbs mixture (available from Nashville House) to taste. Let the slaw set at least one hour in refrigerator before serving.

Overlook Restaurant and Lounge
LEAVENWORTH

1153 W. State Road 62   (812) 739-4264

Open daily April–October 8 A.M.–9 P.M., November–March
8 A.M.–8 P.M. Closed December 24 and 25

If you prefer your fried chicken with a view, then the Overlook off
State Road 62 in deep southern Crawford County is worthy of your
attention. For what the Overlook overlooks is the Ohio River as it
snakes and meanders its way through the Oxbow Bend section; the
Overlook diner can see four alternating views of Indiana and Kentucky in all their wooded splendor and agricultural might.

It was the Overlook's steady customers who gave the restaurant
its current name as they gazed at the wondrous view. Originally it
was dubbed the O-HI-View. When Russell and Ellen Breeden started
a chicken and egg hatchery in 1929—a year notable for the crash of
the stock market—they deemed it wise to augment their hatchery
business with a general store and small café on the second floor, and
gasoline pumps in front.

The Breedens chose a bluff 350 feet above the Ohio, less for its
stunning 25-mile panoramic view than for the high ground that
would keep their businesses safe and dry whenever the Ohio over-
flowed its banks. Down below, the main community of Leavenworth
functioned as a small, bustling river port, founded in 1818 by
brothers Seth and Zebulon Leavenworth as a pit stop for flatboats,
keelboats, and packets transporting meats, produce, spirits, and
lumber. It supported several businesses, eating places, a bank, and a
general store. For over 50 years, Leavenworth was the Crawford
County seat, until English assumed that title.

The January 1937 flood proved to be the last straw for most
of Leavenworth's citizens. With their homes and businesses sub-
merged, residents looked to the foresight and wisdom of the Breedens up on the bluff, and decided to join them. Thus the town of
Leavenworth was rebuilt across the street from the egg hatchery,
leaving the old town to a handful of stubborn, hardy traditionalists.

Meanwhile, the Breedens' hatchery business continued to grow,
necessitating the construction of a larger facility. The old structure,
with its general store, café, and gas station, evolved into a Grey-

hound bus stop, attracting a new batch of hungry visitors and tourists. In 1948, the Breedens sold the store and café to Marjorie Pate and Flora McFall, and Flora brought her cherished fried chicken recipe to the cozy 32-seat café. The combination of stunning view and good food soon made the O-HI-View one of southern Indiana's premier destination eateries.

Succeeding owners Sam and Hilda Reily and Dr. and Mrs. James McClintock maintained its charm over the next four decades, until in 1989 the Overlook Restaurant came full circle as the Breeden family again assumed command—namely Russell and Ellen's three sons and their wives, Doug and Josie Breeden, Russell, Jr. and Annabelle Breeden, and John and Karen Breeden. The driving force is Doug, who is trying to develop his hometown of 350 residents into a genuine tourist mecca and historic site in his belief that the tourist potential of the Hoosier side of the Ohio has never really been tapped. Two homes on the Breeden family estate across from the restaurant have been turned into bed-and-breakfast operations, and a casual bar-restaurant called the Dock operates in old Leavenworth down by the river, now primarily a campground. The hatchery was closed and dismantled after 1982 with Russ Sr.'s retirement, and one of the side buildings was converted into a gift shop and book store.

The Breedens have remodeled the Overlook to achieve a more rustic look using beams from a nearby barn and expanded the seating to 225 in two levels, complete with a party room and an outdoor deck furnished with rocking chairs from which patrons can gaze dreamily at the comforting sight of barges transporting their bulky cargo in that refreshingly unhurried "we'll get there when we get there" spirit while digesting their country-accented fried chicken, beef Manhattan, smoked country ham and pork chops, creamed chicken, skillet-fried chicken livers, catfish, and steaks. And while a 225-seat restaurant for a town that barely exceeds 350 may strike some as overkill, the Overlook is used to having a lot of friends from out of town over for dinner, including 1,100 on a typical Mother's Day. It is open for all three meals every day except Christmas Eve and Christmas Day, bakes its own rolls and cornbread, and dwells at length over the seductive charms of its fruit pies, cobblers, and coconut cream pies, in seeking to fully achieve its trademark boast that it is the "High Point in Dining along the Ohio."

CREAMED CHICKEN

1 stick margarine
1 cup flour
1 pint milk
1 quart chicken stock,
    seasoned to taste

2 teaspoons curry powder
1½ pounds pulled chicken
2 ounces mushrooms
1 ounce pimientos

In a saucepan, melt margarine and flour to make a paste. Add chicken stock and milk. Add remaining ingredients. Cook until it thickens. Serve over your favorite homemade biscuits.

FRENCH DRESSING

13-ounce can tomato soup
¾ cup sugar
⅛ cup Worcestershire sauce
½ tablespoon onion powder
1 tablespoon dry mustard

½ tablespoon paprika
1 cup salad oil
¾ tablespoon celery seeds
¼ tablespoon garlic salt
½ cup vinegar

Use an electric mixer to mix the above ingredients.

Phil Smidt's

HAMMOND

1205 N. Calumet Ave.   (219) 659-0025, 1-800-376-4534

Open for lunch and dinner daily

Phil Smidt's, a Lake County and Chicagoland dining classic since 1910, would never have seen the light of day had not Phil and his bride, Marie, missed the train to California, where they were heading in 1900 to start a new life. Their train from the East Coast had stopped briefly for water in Roby, Indiana, a small town near Hammond. Believing that they were in Chicago, where they were supposed to change trains, the Smidts disembarked and were left behind.

So the two native New Jerseyites put down roots in Roby, and Phil took a grueling job loading blocks of ice on railroad cars at nearby Lake Wolf, a popular recreation area dotted with food shacks serving fried fish, chicken, and sandwiches. Seeing Lake

Wolf, Smidt was inspired to conclude that Roby could also use a good restaurant and tavern specializing in fried lake perch, commercially caught on Lake Michigan and prepared according to Marie's recipe. A friend loaned them $600, and on May 30, 1910, Smidt's Fish and Chicken Dinners was unveiled, offering "all you want" fried perch, rye bread, and a vegetable for 40 cents in a 12-seat, 3-table dining room with a 12-foot bar.

Smidt was able to pay off the loan in two months. Locals flocked there to commune with Marie's pan-fried perch, chicken, steaks, and frog legs. Years later, after Marie Smidt died in 1926, Phil turned the restaurant over to his son, Pete, and his wife, Irene, and it was under the charismatic leadership of Irene Smidt that Phil Smidt's really hit its stride. Insisting on nonstop cleanliness in the kitchen and mother-hen service from the wait staff, she personally fawned over each family, doting on their kids, providing dinghy transportation to those arriving by yacht, hiring boys to clean the windshields of patrons' cars in the parking lot, and extending charity to the community by donating food and money to orphanages, churches, and retirement homes. Pete Smidt was basically in charge of charming and schmoozing, regaling guests in the bar with tales of his golf, hunting, and fishing expeditions.

Smidt's growing reputation attracted sports and entertainment personalities passing through Chicago. On any given night in the '30s and '40s, Babe Ruth, Jack Dempsey, Dizzy Dean, or Bob Hope might be among the customers disposing of plates of perch and/or frog legs.

On January 19, 1945, the explosion of an underground gas pipe at the start of the dinner hour destroyed the restaurant, killing two customers and injuring 19. A year later, Smidt's was reborn at its current location in the former Lundgren's Restaurant on Calumet Avenue in Hammond, in the shadow of the massive Lever Brothers plant, near the shore of Lake Michigan. By now, the sautéed and fried frog legs had achieved marquee status along with the perch, and Smidt's continued to grow and prosper under Irene's steady hand and attention to detail.

Irene's death in January 1969 sent Smidt's into a brief decline. Pete retired, deeding the restaurant to Calumet College. The school struggled to maintain quality in the late '70s at a time of chronic economic woes in the Region, but found the administrative challenges overwhelming until they recruited food service professional Michael Probst as Smidt's manager. Having restored its luster, Probst purchased the restaurant in 1980 in partnership with his younger brother, Chris. The brothers Probst and their staff of 75 superintend seven dining rooms with seating for 450, with an extensive banquet, meeting, and party trade. They are particularly popular for family reunions, where new generations are exposed to the Phil Smidt dining experience.

The "all-you-can-eat" feature of past menus has become cost prohibitive. The perch no longer comes from Lake Michigan due to commercial fishing bans on the Great Lakes, and the frog legs are imported from Indonesia. Fried chicken, steaks, and an extensive array of pan-fried and broiled seafood round out the menu. But the perch and frog legs are still favorites, and the portions more than suffice for the typical diner.

The lobby contains a large framed photograph of the founding father, Phil Smidt. It portrays a robust, white-haired gentleman with a beaming smile, looking for all the world like a successful Lake County Democrat who has just won a landslide reelection victory. Undoubtedly Mr. Smidt felt like smiling often after missing that train and opening that restaurant in Roby. After all, he was doing what most successful politicians do—keep their constituents satisfied and stuffed.

GRILLED LOBSTER

1½ pound lobster	1½ tablespoons Worcestershire
1½ cup olive oil	sauce
½ cup melted butter	1 teaspoon chopped garlic
juice of 2 lemons	salt and pepper to taste

Prepare lobster by splitting and cleaning it. Crack open the claws. Combine remaining ingredients in a bowl. Grill lobster halves shell down, brushing the sauce frequently into the cavities. Be careful that the butter mixture does not spill over the flame, causing more intense heat that in turn will burn the shell of the lobster. When the shells turn bright red, in 5–10 minutes, turn lobster halves meat side down and grill 4–5 minutes longer. Turn again with the meat side up.

When lobster meat is white, the lobster is done. Serve immediately.

PINTO BEANS

1 pound dried pinto beans
¼ pound bacon
3 garlic cloves, halved
1 medium-sized onion, sliced in
    quarters

12 fresh sage leaves or whole
    dried sage leaves, wrapped
    tightly in cheesecloth
2 tablespoons ham base
Salt and pepper to taste
Olive oil
Chives, chopped

Place beans in a large pot. Add water to cover by at least 3". Sauté bacon separately until done. Drain off excess grease and add grease to beans. Add the garlic, onions, sage leaves, and ham base. Bring to a simmer, and simmer gently until tender, about 1 hour. Drain and season to taste with salt and black pepper. Prior to serving, grill sea bass. Warm up pinto beans and place enough to cover the bottom of the plate.

Serve topped with portion of grilled sea bass. Sprinkle with chives.

Red Geranium
NEW HARMONY

504 North Street   (812) 682-4431

Open Tuesday–Saturday 11 A.M.–10 P.M.,
Sunday 11 A.M.–8 P.M.

The Red Geranium had its start as a tea room in a small log house in historic New Harmony, where in 1814 George Rapp and a dissenting German religious group had set up a communal and spiritual utopian society on 20,000 acres of land along the Wabash River in Posey County. Ten years later, having decided to move the "Rappites" to Pennsylvania, Rapp sold the town to Welsh business-man and social reformer Robert Owen who, with partner William McClure, envisioned a community of intellectual and spiritual equality where scientists, scholars, and educators from around the world would gather to discuss social problems and develop reforms. It was Owen who gave his dream community the name New Har-mony, and the ideas developed here had national impact on the development of the public school system, women's suffrage, art, architecture, and industry.

While Owen's utopian experiments did not survive into the 20th century, Jane Blaffer Owen took it upon herself to preserve the memory and spirit of New Harmony's past. She is the widow of Kenneth Owen, the great-great-grandson of Robert Owen, and in the early '60s she funded the preservation and restoration of houses and other buildings of the Rappite and Owens eras. In the ensuing years, she invited prominent architects to design structures emulating the forward thinking of Robert Owen, resulting in Phillip Johnson's Roofless Church and Richard Meier's startlingly modernistic and resoundingly white Atheneum.

Jane Blaffer Owen also built the New Harmony Inn to serve as a hotel, conference center, and retreat, for which the Red Geranium provides dining sustenance in support of all the food for thought generated by the Inn. For, from that tea room in the log cabin, the Red Geranium quickly blossomed into a much-expanded fine-dining restaurant with seating for 175. The main dining room and bar offer the rustic charms of its 19th century roots. A winsome, glass-windowed dining area, built in 1968, overlooks a man-made lake in a well-sculpted park dedicated to the late German theologian Paul Tillich, who was as enamored with the history, spirit, and serenity of New Harmony as Jane Blaffer Owen and whose ashes are interred at this site.

The Red Geranium menu wields a continental flair, with prime rib, Italian pepper steak, beef Stroganoff, and chateaubriand highlighting the beef trust, along with such distinctive entrées as veal Cordon Bleu, sautéed calves' livers, grilled duck breast, Cornish hen in orange glaze, lobster, and that cream-sauced seafood triumph, coquilles Saint-Jacques. A more casual, sandwich-friendly menu is found at the nearby Bayou Grill, built in 1986, seating 300.

The Red Geranium's large staff can count on being worn to a small frazzle on Thanksgiving and Mother's Day, when over 1,000 folks and their mothers pop in for dinner. And through the year, especially in the summer and fall, diners from all over the country come to break bread after communing with one of the most intriguing, reflective, and spiritual stops on the Midwest tourist circuit.

CAESAR STEAK

2 pounds beef tenderloin (in 1½ inch slices)
6 ounces olive oil
2 tablespoons garlic powder

8 ounces burgundy wine
seasoned salt
seasoned flour
12 ounces beef broth

Heat olive oil in heavy skillet. Flour meat slices heavily and sear on both sides in oil. Sauté for approximately 3 minutes for medium. Add a pinch of seasoned salt and drain off the oil. Add garlic powder, rubbing into the meat with spoon. Add beef broth and wine. Reduce until the sauce thickens and serve over the steak.

Note: To prevent overcooking the steak, it may be removed from the sauce before the sauce has finished cooking.

SHAKER LEMON PIE

5 small lemons, with seeds removed and rind cut off
2 cups granulated sugar
5 eggs, beaten well

1 full pie crust
1 tablespoon melted butter
1 tablespoon Milnot
pastry for 2 crusts

In a large bowl, combine sliced lemons and sugar, mixing until sugar is dissolved. Let stand, covered, overnight. Add beaten eggs to lemon and sugar mixture. Mix well. Pour into bottom crust, cover with top crust, and seal the sides well. Insert small holes in top crust for baking. Brush melted butter over the top crust.

Bake at 250° in convection oven or 300° in conventional oven for 1 hour and 10 minutes. Increase oven temperature by 50° and remove pie from the oven. Brush a thin layer of Milnot over the top crust and return pie to oven. Bake until crust becomes light brown.

Cool pie so that it develops a thicker consistency. Warm slightly before serving.

St. Elmo Steak House

INDIANAPOLIS

127 S. Illinois Street   (317) 635-0636

Open Monday–Saturday 4–10:30 P.M., Sunday 5–9:30 P.M.

St. Elmo Steak House was founded in 1902, and through most of the 20th century it enjoyed a reputation among both local citizenry and visitors as *the* place in Indy for steaks. A century later, it no longer has the beef trust to itself; prominent upscale national steak chains have put down roots in the Mile Square. But St. Elmo, still in its original location at 127 South Illinois Street, remains Indianapolis' best known restaurant nationally.

A major component of its success is the simple fact that there have been few departures from the game plan and ambience created by its founding father, Joe Stahr. Stahr had an interest in all things nautical, which explains why he named his establishment after the patron saint of sailors, and perhaps why he lavished so much attention on the shrimp cocktail, which never failed to get a St. Elmo repast off to a dynamic start: he swamped the shrimp in a horserad-ish-endowed cocktail sauce with the medicinal capabilities to clear diners' sinuses and melt their earwax.

St. Elmo's was the quintessential gaslight-era saloon steak house. We can envision tuxedoed waiters with handlebar mustaches and center-parted hair fetching big drinks and big steaks for guys who think, drink, and eat big. One can assume that more than a few business and political deals were hatched and sealed on the premises.

Little in St. Elmo's ambience or decor changed when the retiring Stahr sold the restaurant in 1946 to the dynamic duo of Harry Roth and Isadore Rosen. On the surface, they were an odd couple, with the fussily attentive Roth, resplendent in black-rimmed glasses, bow tie, and polka dot shirt, contrasting with the stogie-smoking, laid-back Rosen, garbed in rumpled, open-collar Ban-Lon shirt. But they made a good team.

The action began at the front door, with a long oak bar on the right and broilers on the left, right behind the meat case. Customers stacked up at the door were in effect led to their table through the kitchen and the bar amid waiters nimbly weaving and pirouetting with trays of shrimp cocktails, lettuce wedge salads, and hefty cuts of prime beef.

For many years, St. Elmo was that relatively rare restaurant that drew greater crowds on week nights than weekends; it attracted local and traveling businessmen with clients and generous expense accounts as well as scores of entertainers, athletes, coaches, and politicians, who were enticed by the owners to leave an autographed 8x10 glossy as a memento. The bar area and hallway are adorned with photos of the chronically famous, past and present. Harry Roth's photo with Angie Dickinson is particularly prized.

Roth and Rosen guided St. Elmo through the rocky shoals of major downtown economic decline in the '60s. Making a major effort through advertising to attract the local citizenry, St. Elmo persevered during that period when a bowling ball could be rolled down Washington Street or Monument Circle after 6 P.M. without fear of striking anyone downtown in pursuit of nightlife, and was poised to fully embrace Indianapolis' downtown renaissance when it began in the '80s.

After 40 years, Roth and Rosen retired in 1986, selling St. Elmo to Jeff Dunaway, a former waiter, and Stephen Huse, a founding father of the Noble Roman's chain. The opening of Circle Centre mall in the mid-'90s generated a second downtown restaurant invasion of popular chains, notably the bistros Palomino and California Café, such youth-magnet theme eateries as Hard Rock Café, Jillian's, and the now-extinct Planet Hollywood, and no less than three prime beef emporiums—Ruth's Chris, Shula's in the Weston Hotel, and Morton's of Chicago—all challenging the venerable St. Elmo. This competition inspired Huse, the controlling partner, to give St. Elmo a major fashion makeover, leading to the departure of Dunaway in a contentious dispute that was resolved in an out-of-court settlement. The restaurant was renovated and expanded into four dining rooms, with a spacious open kitchen in the rear where a back dining nook once prevailed. Replacing the old broiler location at the front entrance is a small cocktail area. A party and meeting room on the basement level has a view of the well-stocked wine cellar.

The menu pretty much remains as it was in 1902: imposing cuts of New York strip, filets, rib-eyes, and a 28-ounce prime rib, with pork and veal chops, lobster, salmon, and walleye in the supporting cast. Huse also offers desserts in the interest of full service, unlike his predecessors who basically felt a St. Elmo steak left no room for dessert. And yes, that memorable shrimp cocktail is still potent after all these years—symbolic of the staying power of St. Elmo.

CHEDDAR MASHED REDSKINS

1 tablespoon kosher salt	2 cups crumbled cheddar cheese
1 tablespoon black pepper	2 cups sour cream
1/2 cup butter, melted	1/4 cup fresh parsley, finely chopped
1 cup half-and-half, heated	8 pounds redskin potatoes

Steam the potatoes to tenderness, and immediately place in large mixing bowl. Combine the potatoes with the remaining ingredients. Mash and serve.

Sprinkle additional fresh parsley on top of mashed potatoes after they are plated.

CREAMED SPINACH

2 pounds butter
1 gallon finely chopped onion
$\frac{1}{2}$ cup garlic, minced by hand
28 ounces canned artichoke
   hearts, slightly chopped
6 quarts heavy cream
1$\frac{1}{2}$ cups fresh lemon juice
3 cups Parmesan cheese, chopped
   fine

4 quarts sour cream
$\frac{1}{3}$ cup Tabasco sauce
36 pounds spinach, frozen and
   chopped
2 tablespoons salt
2 tablespoons black pepper
4 tablespoons sugar

Sauté onion and minced garlic in butter until tender. Remove from heat and combine with remaining ingredients. Mix well. Portion into microwave-safe small serving bowls. Cover with plastic wrap and refrigerate. Microwave individual servings for 2 minutes. Stir before serving

Sarge Oak on Main
LAFAYETTE

721 Main Street   (765) 742-5230

Open for lunch Tuesday–Friday 11:30 am.–2 P.M., for dinner Tuesday–Saturday 4:30–9:30 P.M. (kitchen closes 9:45 P.M. Fri.–Sat.)

It is somewhat difficult to spot Sarge Oak on Main, what with two large trees blocking its sign. But those on the quest for the best steaks in Lafayette instinctively know to go there. They are enamored not only of its hefty filets, strips, porterhouses, and rib-eyes, but of its colorful, decidedly checkered past.

What began life in 1933 as the Black Hawk Café was won three years later in a poker game by entrepreneur Rholdo Ghere. Ghere soon redubbed it the Oak Tavern, in honor of its oak bar. He came close to losing said oak bar, as well as the lovely red velvet drapes, when a creditor swooped down to claim them in payment of a longstanding $200 debt. Ghere quickly peeled off a couple of century notes and saved the oak bar and drapes. Both still endure today.

In that period of Lafayette's past, it enjoyed a raucous, river-town reputation as the "Wettest Town on the Wabash," with distilleries and speakeasies flourishing through the purse-lipped objections of Prohibition. Not only was the Oak Tavern a reliable watering hole, but it was one of many downtown businesses with a back room for such above-the-law investment opportunities as poker, roulette, and craps. Ghere's gambling operations were friendly affairs; he would reimburse women whose husbands gambled away the food money with the understanding that said spouses would not darken the back room again. A light bulb behind the bar flashed to alert the bartender that the boys in the back would like another round of drinks. A light bulb in the back room flashed to warn the boys that this would be a good time to take a stroll out the rear door and get some air, since assorted authority figures had just entered the premises on official business.

In the late '40s Ghere, noticing that his clientele were compelled to take their dinner breaks at competing establishments and sometimes not returning, decided to offer food as well as fuel. Coming to his culinary rescue (reportedly roaring in on a motorcycle from Ohio) was one Sidney Sargent, a former professional wrestler during a period when that discipline was considered a sport, not a Hulk Hogan morality play. Mr. Sargent asserted that he was well acquainted with the fine art of cutting and cooking large hunks of red meat, and Ghere rented out his kitchen to Sargent for a dollar a day.

So acclaimed were Sidney Sargent's steaks that he and his wife, Josephine, opened a dining room next to the Oak Tavern, Sargent's Fine Food. In 1962, he purchased the Oak Tavern, running restaurant and bar as separate business operations to show skeptics that each could prosper on its own. Sargent was a man of high standards and strong opinions that rarely went unexpressed, especially regarding his steaks. First seared in a hot skillet, which produced a crusty top to lock in the juices, they were then chargrilled from rare to medium—never beyond. A waitress's routine inquiry, "How would you like that cooked?" was strictly rhetorical at Sargent's. Chef Sidney passionately believed optimum goodness could only be achieved at the level of "medium rare." It was not all that unusual for customers to be treated to the sight of Sargent emerging from the kitchen with cleaver in hand and garbed in a blood-streaked white apron to debate a stubborn carnivore with "well-done" theories about beef preparedness.

And in the late '60s, with the dawn of the Woodstock generation, many a beleaguered waitress would contrive to keep Sargent back in the kitchen so that he wouldn't notice the table of male Purdue students sprouting long, flowing locks. Long hair on men was an affront to Sargent's fashion and gender senses, and a sign of rebellion he was always prepared to quash. But most customers enjoyed his opinionated ways.

Sidney Sargent passed away in 1970, but Josephine carried on through the rest of the decade. Retiring in 1980, she sold the restaurant and bar to its current owners, Mel and Grace Ann Brutsman, who formally combined the two operations to become Sarge Oak on Main. They have skillfully guided the restaurant through a dicey period of downtown economic decline and renewal, expanding the menu to include more seafood and chicken but remaining true to and focused on Sidney Sargent's beef legacy. They take pains to cook steaks the way the Sarge did, while bringing the concepts of diplomacy, tolerance, and graciousness to the table in granting—Sidney Sargent would say surrendering to—the customers' wishes on how they should be prepared.

SARGE OAK CELERY SEED DRESSING

1 small onion, minced
1 cup sugar
1 teaspoon dry mustard
2 teaspoons celery seed

½ cup plus 2 teaspoons cider vinegar
2 cups good salad oil

Mix together onion, sugar, dry mustard, celery seed, and cider vinegar, adding the salad oil slowly. Continue mixing until it is all well blended.

GRACE ANN'S CHOCOLATE AMARETTO PIE (6–8 servings)

¼ cup (half a stick) unsalted butter
½ cup unsweetened cocoa powder
1 cup (2 sticks) unsalted butter at room temperature

1½ cups superfine sugar
¼ cup amaretto liquer
4 eggs, room temperature
1 9" deep-dish pie crust, baked

Melt ¼ cup butter in heavy small saucepan, then remove from heat.

Stir in the cocoa powder. Cream one cup of butter with sugar and amaretto in large electric mixer bowl. Gradually beat in cocoa mixture. Add eggs one at a time, beating for 3 minutes after each addition. Continue beating until sugar is completely dissolved. Pour into crust. Cover and refrigerate until firm, about 4 hours.

Shapiro's Delicatessen
INDIANAPOLIS

808 S. Meridian St.   (317) 631-4041

Open daily 6:30 A.M.–8:30 P.M.

2370 W. 86th St.   (317) 872-7255

Open daily 6:30 A.M.–8:30 P.M.

"Cook good, serve generous, price modestly, and people will come." These words to live and nosh by have been the guiding philosophy of Shapiro's Delicatessen and Cafeteria since 1905. More than 2,000 customers drop in each day for breakfast, lunch, and dinner at its two locations. It is far and away Indiana's, and many would argue the Midwest's, prime forum for corned beef and pastrami piled high on rye or egg bun and for matzo ball and chicken noodle soups, and for such comfort foods as Swiss steak, baked chicken, meat loaf, macaroni and cheese, and unconscionably high-rise pies, cakes, and pastries. And it is perhaps the last Hoosier haven for smoked pickled tongue.

This is not exactly what Louis and Rebecca Shapiro had in mind when they opened their tiny grocery-deli in 1905, eight blocks south of downtown Indianapolis. The Shapiros were just two years removed from their native Russia, where Louis' grandfather was a primary food supplier for the Czar's naval fleet, and where Louis operated a grocery in Odessa named to reflect his career ambitions, the American Grocery Company. The anti-Jewish pogroms that erupted in Russia at the turn of the century meant that Louis was spending many nights fending off vandals while Rebecca and the children hid in the basement. The Shapiros emigrated to America in

1903, settling in Indianapolis. After raising capital through push-cart street sales of flour and sugar, they set up shop at Meridian and McCarty streets, with living quarters above the store for themselves and their eight children. The Shapiros saw to it that the grocery was a family affair, waking the children at 3 each morning with the rallying cry, "The day is half over already!"

The grocery featured canned goods stacked in dazzling pyramid displays, pickles and mayonnaise, and kosher deli meats supplied by the Vienna Meat Company out of Chicago. The transition to restaurant began after the end of Prohibition in the mid-'30s, when the aging Louis, suffering from back problems, delegated the running of the store to sons Abe, Izzy, and Max. They started selling beer for ten cents a bottle, and before long customers were ordering salami (29 cents) and corned beef (10 cents) sandwiches to go with the brew. That brought about the appearance of tables and chairs. The next thing they knew, the Shapiros were installing a steam table to showcase Rebecca's dinner triumphs, notably her spaghetti and meatballs.

Their timing proved exquisite. The surrounding ethnic neighborhood was giving way to industrial expansion and general migration north, dooming Shapiro's prospects as a full-service grocery but enhancing its repuation as a destination deli. In 1940 Louis formally retired, anointing Izzy to handle the deli counter, Abe, with his award-winning corned beef recipe, to preside over the kitchen, and bon-vivant Max, a dedicated bachelor, to oversee the whole operation. A photograph in the restaurant shows Louis surrounded by his five grown sons, with Max looking like he's about to head off to the Stork Club, decked out in a double-breasted suit, boutonnière, and spats. Indeed, even in a sauce-stained apron, Max Shapiro was the essense of dapper and debonair.

Max served as major domo of Shapiro's for 44 years, even as his bachelorhood came to a halt in his 50s. He guided Shapiro's through several expansions, including a kitchen and bakery that could fully accommodate the preparation of its minimum daily requirement of 300 pounds of the steam-cooked corned beef briskets; 100 pounds each of pastrami, turkey, and roast beef; 150 to 200 loaves of rye bread, and the quartering of 1,000 pickles. During this period, Max kept vacations to a minimum, figuring each day was a schmoozefest with good friends over good eats. Nor did the word "retirement" find its way into his vocabulary; he continued to supervise Shapiro's past his 80th birthday.

His two marriages relatively late in life produced no children, but he ensured continuing Shapiro leadership by enticing his nephew, businessman and investment banker Mort Shapiro, and Mort's son Brian, fresh from law school, to join the firm in 1984. Thus, they were in place when Max died suddenly in October 1984. Shortly before, they had convinced Max of the wisdom of opening a second Shapiro's off West 86th Street and Township Line Road on the northwestside, and it was an immediate and lasting success. Perfectionist Max had resisted such expansion despite the entreaties of his northside clientele with the heartfelt if dubious explanation, "Why should I open a second restaurant when I still haven't got the first one off the ground?"

Mort, handling books and payroll, and Brian, running day-to-day operations with an uncompromising insistence on quality, saw to it that both locations ran on all cylinders as Indiana's premier and most productive deli operation. Mort's death in 1999 invested Brian with the full mantle of fourth-generation leadership of Shapiro's, now in its second century of cooking well, serving generously, pricing moderately, and watching customers continue to come.

STUFFED CABBAGE (serves 6)

2 medium-sized heads cabbage
1 pound lean ground chuck
$\frac{1}{2}$ cup finely chopped onion
1 rib celery, finely chopped
1 egg, beaten
3 slices white bread soaked in $\frac{1}{3}$ cup red wine
$\frac{1}{4}$ cup tomato juice
1 cup cooked rice
1 teaspoon salt

$\frac{1}{2}$ teaspoon black pepper
2 cups stewed tomatoes
$\frac{1}{2}$ cup tomato puree
1 cup water
$\frac{1}{2}$ cup brown sugar
juice of 1 lemon
6 gingersnap cookies, about 2 inches in diameter
$\frac{1}{2}$ cup golden raisins

For cabbage and beef: Core the cabbage and blanch in a large pot of boiling water until the leaves begin to loosen. Combine the ground chuck, onion, celery, and egg. Mix in the wine-soaked bread, preferably with bare hands. Add tomato juice, rice, salt, and pepper. Carefully peel off the cabbage leaves and roll each around 1–2 tablespoons of the meat mixture, tucking in the sides so it holds together. Repeat until all the beef is wrapped. There should be 18 to 20 packets. Chop remaining cabbage leaves and reserve 4 cups.

For sauce and assembly instructions: In a large stock pot, heat stewed tomatoes, puree, water, brown sugar, and lemon juice. Crumble ginger snaps and stir into mixture. Stir in raisins and chopped cabbage leaves. Add salt and pepper to taste, if desired. Carefully add stuffed cabbage packets to the sauce

Cover well and cook over medium-low heat for 1 hour and 15 minutes. Check occasionally and add $\frac{1}{4}$ to $\frac{1}{2}$ cup tomato juice to the sauce if it appears to be drying out.

FLOURLESS CHOCOLATE TORTE

For the torte:

4 ounces water	7 whole eggs
7 ounces sugar	6 ounces sugar
5$\frac{1}{2}$ ounces semisweet chocolate	dash salt
3$\frac{1}{2}$ ounces bitter chocolate (no sugar)	2 ounces vanilla extract
	8 ounces finely ground pecans
2 sticks butter, melted	

ganache sauce:

1 pint heavy cream	4 ounces bitter chocolate
1 pound semi-sweet chocolate	

For the torte: Combine water and 7 ounces of sugar, and bring to a boil. Add semi-sweet and bitter chocolates until melted. Add the melted butter. In mixing bowl place eggs, 6 ounces of sugar, salt, and vanilla, and whip to a peak. Take fine-ground pecans and add to egg mixture, then fold into chocolate mixture. Grease 10" round x 2" high cake pan. Line bottom of pan with parchment paper. Pour batter into pan and bake at 300° in a water bath for 45–55 minutes. The cake will still be very moist and fudgy. Refrigerate overnight. After refrigeration, remove from cake pan. Top with ganache sauce.

For ganache sauce: Bring to boil 1 pint heavy cream. Add 1 pound semi-sweet chocolate and 4 ounces bitter chocolate. Let cool approximately 30 minutes to allow mixture to thicken.

Put cake on wire rack and pour ganache sauce over the cake, distributing with spatula to cover the entire top and sides. Apply ground pecans to sides of the cake. Garnish with a dollop of whipped cream, fresh raspberries, and any type of fruit sauce.

Story Inn
STORY

6404 S. State Road 135   (812) 988-2273, (800) 881-1183

Open for breakfast, lunch, and dinner Tuesday–Sunday

Tiny Story is about 12 miles south of Nashville via an exhilarating stretch of State Road 135, complete with roller coaster hills and hairpin turns. Its transformation from 1970s ghost town to modern-day gourmet restaurant/bed & breakfast destination represents one of Indiana's most remarkable historic reclamation projects.

At one time, Story (then called Storyville) was Brown County's largest and liveliest settlement, fueled by an active timber industry begun in the 1850s by the town's founder, Dr. George Story. In its salad days, from the late 1880s to the early 1920s, Storyville supported two general stores, a sawmill, a slaughterhouse, a blacksmith shop, a post office, a nondenominational church, and a one-room schoolhouse. A prominent entrepreneur in the village was Alra Wheeler, who took over the main general store from Dr. Story's son, George, in the late 1800s. The store was destroyed by fire in 1915, but was rebuilt and expanded by Wheeler the next year as a two-story structure, with the general store on the ground floor and the upper floor given over to a Studebaker Company buggy assembly operation. Storyville became just plain Story in 1917 when the U.S. Post Office took root in the general store, with Alra Wheeler serving as postmaster.

Story's boom ended in the early '20s thanks to Colonel Richard Lieber, who was crusading to establish what would become Brown County State Park on land immediately north of Story. With several citizens served by Story forced to move, and the resulting cutback in available timber resources, the town underwent a rapid decline, exacerbated by the sudden death of Wheeler in 1922. Wheeler's family sold the general store that same year to the duo of John Morrison and Richard Kelly, who unloaded it three years later to Albert "Pink" Hedrick, who ran it with his daughter Clotha Hedrick Robertson for the next 44 years, as the last vestige of a bygone age. By 1969, the Story General Store had seemingly breathed its last, lying dormant with several other wooden homesteads from Story's storied past.

Then, in the mid-'70s, a young couple immersed in sentiments of the Woodstock generation literally took over the town. Cindy and Benjamin Schultz brought the vision of a gourmet restaurant and bed and breakfast complex. Schultz, a building contractor who went by the single name of "Benjamin," remodeled the general store, maintaining its weathered façade, putting four guest bedrooms on the second floor and the restaurant on the main level, offering a natural-foods gourmet touch for all three meals on the main floor. The restaurant was festooned with the antique farm implements, horse fashion wear, and commercial pantry and kitchen products that were the stock in trade of the Story General Store, complete with the obligatory pot-bellied stove. The creaky porch features a traditional Brown County "liar's bench" for post-meal digestion, tall stories, and philosophical digressions, flanked by the regal glass-crowned Red and Gold Crown gas pumps. Subsequently most of the other buildings in town, including the ancestral estate of the founder, Dr. Story, were transformed into guest cottages. Cindy and Benjamin's creative ways with omelettes, steaks, fresh seafood, lamb, veal, chicken, and pasta helped put Story back on the map, drawing folks from throughout central Indiana, tourists on their annual Brown County fall frolic, and many arriving by steed after a judicious gallop through the adjoining Brown County State Forest.

The Schultzes sold the Story Inn in 1994 to Robert and Gretchen Haddix, who were able to maintain the food quality and gracious service, but ultimately encountered financial problems trying to deal with the maintenance headaches even buildings built to last produce in their dotage. Thus it came to pass in December 1998 that the Story Inn was purchased by chef Frank Mueller and businessman Rick Hofstetter, both armed with lofty ambitions for the town.

The German-born Mueller, best known for his achievements at the Rathskeller Restaurant in Indianapolis' Athenaeum Turners building, has kept the Story Inn legacy flourishing with creative breakfast omelettes and banana-walnut hotcakes; lunchtime grilled artichoke croissants, Celtic sausage, and turkey Waldorf sandwiches; and rotating dinner entrées such as French-cut lamb chops, Kentucky bourbon strip steaks, and pork medallions, plus a nightly fresh fish special.

The guest rooms total a dozen—five in the Inn, seven in the neighboring cottages. All lack televisions, radios, or telephones in the belief that those who journey back in time to Story, Indiana are looking for a respite from the present. Those who must have MTV or ESPN can head next door to the Old Mill Bar and Grill, resurrected in the summer of '99 for sandwiches, libations, gourmet coffee, bakery items, and access to the outside world via the satellite dish. As the name suggests, the building once served as the town's flour mill. Across the street is a country-crafted gift shop. An old barn and backyard property are being restored for the purpose of staging outdoor music festivals, plays, poetry readings, receptions, parties, and other group activities.

BANANA-WALNUT PANCAKES

Dry ingredients:
4–5 cups white flour
4 cups whole wheat flour
3 tablespoons baking powder
1$\frac{1}{2}$ tablespoons baking soda
1$\frac{1}{2}$ tablespoons salt
1 cup wheat germ (optional)

Wet ingredients:
8 eggs
1 cup salad oil
8 cups buttermilk
8 mashed bananas
$\frac{3}{4}$ cup honey or sugar

Measure dry ingredients in large bowl and mix with a wire whisk. Measure wet ingredients in a separate bowl, mix well, and then pour in the dry ingredients. Stir until blended. Pour into clean container in preparation for the griddle.

BLEU CHEESE–DILL DRESSING

Place in dressing container, in precise order listed:
2$\frac{1}{2}$ pounds bleu cheese (half a bag)
1$\frac{1}{2}$ cups dried dill weed
1$\frac{1}{2}$ cups dried chives
$\frac{3}{4}$ cup garlic powder
$\frac{1}{4}$ cups or 4 tablespoons white pepper
3 quarts buttermilk

Blend ingredients thoroughly, and then add 1$\frac{1}{2}$ gallons of mayonnaise. Mix well. Add 1–2 cups of buttermilk. Mix until it is pourable.

Strongbow Turkey Inn
VALPARAISO

2405 U.S. 30 East (State Road 49 & U.S. 30)
(219) 462-5121; (800) 462-5121

Open Sunday–Thursday 11 A.M.–9 P.M.,
Friday–Saturday 11 A.M.–10 P.M.

Sometime in the mid-'30s, Bess Thrun picked up a USDA circular
extolling the benefits of raising those all-American, one-size-feeds-
all birds who achieved star billing at the first Thanksgiving and
cornered the market on all the Thanksgivings that followed. Thrun
figured gobbler production would nicely augment the salary of her
husband, Walter, a chemistry professor at Valparaiso University. So
in 1937, she went into partnership with her husband's friend and
academic colleague Harry Fuller to buy a farm, populate it with a
gaggle of turkeys, and name it the Strongbow Turkey Farm after a
local 19th century Potawatomi Indian chief.

All of this coincided with the coast-to-coast construction of U.S.
30, which passed, most fortuitously, right through the Strongbow
Turkey Farm. As automobiles cruised by, their occupants gazed out
the windows at prime specimens of Strongbow turkeyhood. It occurred to Bess Thrun that a journey through the countryside could
make a person hungry, and what better remedy for that hunger than
a roast turkey sandwich? Thus, in 1940, she opened a one-room
eatery called the Strongbow Turkey Inn on the north side of the
road, predictably showcasing turkey sandwiches, and, soon after,
full-scale turkey dinners with all the trimmings, straight from the
source on the south side of the road.

As many have discovered throughout the bountiful history of
Thanksgiving Day, feasting on turkey does not lend itself to a desire
to continue on one's journey when a living room couch beckons.
Given her remote location, Bess had the foresight to put up a series
of cozy cabins in which travelers could stay the night and digest in
comfort. It was Valparaiso's first motel.

Like most operations, the Strongbow Turkey Inn had to struggle through the war years, when gas rationing and labor shortages
sapped business. But the restaurant hit its stride upon war's end,

with an onrush of customers deeming the Strongbow one of their favorite U.S. 30 culinary pit stops, and compelling Mrs. Thrun to indulge in frequent bouts of remodeling and expansion. When speed was of the essence, she would blithely requisition one of the cabins, knock out its front door and windows, and have it pulled smack up against the restaurant for additional space.

Mrs. Thrun retired in 1969, turning the restaurant over to her daughter, Caroline, and her husband, Chuck Adams, and lived to see them turn it into the dining landmark it is today, with seating for 750, lavish banquet facilities, a thriving catering operation, and a winsome pub, festooned with model airplanes to reflect Chuck's passion for aviation. Adams operated the turkey farm for many years, but increasingly tough, complex, and expensive government regulations prompted the family to get out of the gobbler-raising business in 1981. With other companies processing birds to their exacting specifications, they could concentrate on the restaurant. There is today no evidence of the turkey farm across the road.

With their retirement in 1993, Caroline and Chuck passed the inn on to their son, Russ, and his wife, Nancy, taking pains to see that Russ was academically prepared for the challenge. His training and graduation from the Culinary Institute of America permitted him to take this noble bird and its white-meat breast to new continental gourmet vistas heretofore considered the exclusive preserve of veal. Thus, the Strongbow menu shows off chef Russ's depth and versatility with turkey schnitzel, turkey Oscar, turkey Marsala, and turkey Dijon, with beef, seafood, lamb, and veal also making cameo appearances.

But the vast majority of those who have made the Strongbow Inn one of the highest-sales-volume restaurants in Indiana come for a warm, fuzzy repast of sliced turkey breast, dressing, mashed potatoes, and gravy. The comforting, nostalgic flavors are further enhanced by relatively recent disclosures that turkey ranks among our healthiest, most fat-free meats.

A peek into the Strongbow kitchen at one of the 28- to 30-pound birds emerging from the oven does not conjure up Thanksgiving at Grandma's. Minus wings and drumsticks, they are encased in clear cooking bags and placed in large covered iron roasting pans in a little bit of water. There is no obsessive butter basting for photogenic browning, for the white, moist bird is subjected to the carving knife shortly after its session in the oven. And it's an everything-but-the-gobble operation—the wings and drumsticks cooked separately for their own honored place on the menu; the dark meats featured in turkey salads, turkey pâté, and signature turkey pot pie, which is carried by local groceries; the bones, skin, and organs enhancing the flavor of rich turkey soup. A hustling staff of more than a hundred fuss over and serve up, put to the ultimate tests on weekends and holidays—notably on one cherished holiday. Russ Adams figures about 2,500 people come by for supper every Thanksgiving—a day so hectic for the staff that the restaurant is closed the next day for the purposes of recuperation.

STRONGBOW'S TURKEY À LA KING

4 tablespoons butter
1 cup sliced fresh mushroom
1 cup chopped green pepper
4 tablespoons flour
1 teaspoon salt
4 cups milk

6 cups cut-up cooked turkey
½ cup butter
6 egg yolks
1 teaspoon orange juice
2 tablespoons lemon juice
1 teaspoon paprika

Melt the butter and cook the mushrooms and green pepper for ten minutes. Add flour and salt and cook until frothy. Add milk and cook until smooth. Add turkey and cover, keeping it hot. Now cream the butter and egg yolks. Add orange juice, lemon juice, and paprika. Add a little of the hot mixture to the egg yolk mixture and blend, and then return all of this to the hot mixture. Stir over very low heat until eggs are set. Serve in patty shells or over toast points or rice.

STRONGBOW TURKEY SOUP

4 cups diced celery
1 cup minced onion
½ cup butter or margarine
8 cups turkey broth
2 cups finely chopped cooked
  turkey meat

1 cup rice or noodles (cooked
  previously)
½ teaspoons chopped parsley for
  each bowl

Cook celery and onion in butter until transparent and soft, but not brown. Remove from heat and add broth, chopped turkey, and rice and noodles. Garnish each bowl with parsley.

Teibel's Restaurant
SCHERERVILLE

U.S. 30 & U.S. 41   (219) 865-2000

Open Monday–Thursday 11 A.M.–10 P.M.,
Friday–Saturday 11 A.M.–11 P.M., Sunday 11 A.M.–8 P.M.

The opening of Teibel's Restaurant in Schererville basically coincided with the crash of the stock market in 1929. But what brothers Stephen and Martin Teibel lacked in timing, they more than made up for in pluck, perseverance, and—most importantly—vision. Both had been working as proprietors and mechanics at a one-pump gas station in Hammond, but they yearned for the quieter but no less challenging life to be had in rural Indiana. Taking note of the new routes being built by the federal government, among them east-westbound U.S. 30 and north-south U.S. 41, they found that they would intersect off an old Indian trail in Schererville. With an eye toward setting up farm and rural business operations there, they bought the property on two of the corners of the intersection off weather-ravaged dirt roads, and promptly put a 12-seat diner crafted from an old wooden box car on one lot.

Armed with a dynamite fried chicken recipe from their Austrian great-grandmother, Martin and Steve, with their wives Lydia and Marie, doggedly plowed through the Depression with their little diner on the prairie and the chicken coop out back. As U.S. 30 and U.S. 41 finally brought their paved majesty to Schererville, the Teibels' business interests expanded at all four corners of the intersection and beyond, with service stations, a large livestock operation, and a farm implement business in the mix.

But it was the restaurant that was capturing the interest of travelers and locals, allowing the Teibels to replace their tiny wooden diner with a more spacious brick structure in the '30s. The fried chicken seemed to make the deepest impression until, in the late '40s, taking a cue from Phil Smidt's in Hammond, fried lake perch from nearby Lake Michigan made its debut on the menu. With the chicken and perch both ultimately offered on an all-you-can-devour basis, the Teibel family had a bona fide hit that attracted the multitudes on weekends.

And that became the challenge for Steve's son, Harold, and

Martin's son, Robert, when they assumed command in the '50s. They embarked on a major expansion in 1957 that allowed for seating for 650 in four dining rooms, adaptable for wedding receptions, business banquets and meetings, Christmas parties, family reunions, and just plain weekend dinners. This is not to mention the roughly 3,000 folks taking Mom out on Mother's Day because Mom thinks Teibel's chicken is darn near as good as hers. The expansion even included a coffee shop for the area's eat-and-run crowd.

Harold's son, Stephen, and Robert's first-born, Robert Jr., represent the third generation of Teibels. Taking over in 1977, they expanded the restaurant to 800 seats in 1985 to meet the demands of the escalating banquet and catering trade as well as increased competition from the invasion of malls and the usual suspects from the franchise restaurant colony, who discovered in the late '80s that the Teibels might be on to something.

The staff is now up to 130, serving approximately 1,500 lunches and dinners per day. Chicken and perch are still the star attractions, augmented by roast beef, steaks, roast pork, and turkey. With commercial fishing no longer permitted on Lake Michigan, the cherished perch must be imported from Ontario at much higher prices. Its popularity compels the Teibels to fly in 2,000 pounds of perch four times a week, even though it is only fiscally sound to offer it on an all-you-can-eat basis on Friday nights.

There are 11 children in the fourth generation of Teibels available to take over whenever Bob, Jr. and Steve decide to pursue the retirement arts, but so far none appear be chomping at the bit in their wonder years. But their dads figure that may change when they come to fully appreciate what Teibel's has achieved, making pluck, perseverance, and vision pay off.

STUFFED MUSHROOM CAPS

16–18 mushroom caps
1/8 teaspoon salt
1/8 teaspoon pepper
1 cup Swiss cheese, shredded
1 cup Cheddar cheese, shredded
1 cup American cheese, shredded
1/8 cup bacon bits
1/8 cup scallion tops, chopped

Parboil mushrooms until medium soft and allow to drain until as dry as possible. Once dried, arrange the mushroom caps bottom up, on a lightly buttered tray. Season with salt and pepper. Preheat oven to 350°. Mix all the cheeses, bacon bits, and scallion tops together in a mixing bowl. Cover all the mushroom caps completely with the cheese mixture, and bake for 15 minutes, or until all cheese is melted. Serves 2 to 3.

Tippecanoe Place
SOUTH BEND

620 W. Washington St.   (219) 234-9077

Open for lunch Monday–Friday 11:30 A.M.–2 P.M.; for dinner Monday–Friday 5–10 P.M., Saturday 4:30–10:30 P.M.; Sunday 4–9 P.M.; Sunday brunch 9 A.M.–2 P.M.

I think I can say without fear of contradiction that Tippecanoe Place is the stateliest, most majestic restaurant in Indiana. Majestic is pretty much what wagon baron Clement Studebaker had in mind in 1886 when he called upon architect Henry Cobb to design a home reflecting his lofty position in life as president of the Studebaker Brothers Manufacturing Company, makers of quality wagons, where he and his second wife, Ann Milburn Harper, and their children could live and entertain in an appropriate manner. The Civil War had been a boon to the wagon manufacturing business; Clement and his brothers made thousands of them for the Union Army, and soon Clement was able to count such business titans as Andrew Carnegie, J. P. Morgan, Cyrus McCormick, and John Wanamaker as close personal friends. Thus he needed a dwelling befitting his importance.

When Cobb and the area's best craftsmen finished their work in 1889, the Studebakers' dream home stood four stories tall, its massive walls garbed in granite fieldstone, its 26,000 square feet encompassing 40 rooms, 20 fireplaces, a fourth-floor ballroom, massive hardwood doors with decorative carvings on the oval doorknobs, and one of the nation's first elevators. Stone pillars hold up the many porches, paved in tile. The expansive vestibule off the main entrance features lush mahogany paneling and a staircase that gives visitors the feeling that they are making a grand entrance. In the relatively brief period they lived there, the Studebakers threw many a grand soirée.

It was Clement who dubbed his estate Tippecanoe Place, perhaps upon learning that the ground on which his mansion stood was once a favored camping site of Tippecanoe, the chief of the Miami Indians. Another theory is that Clement's friendship with Benjamin Harrison, the 23rd president, may have inspired the name in memory of the Battle of Tippecanoe in 1811, where Benjamin's grandfather, William Henry Harrison, earned his reputation as a military leader with a victory ("Tippecanoe and Tyler Too") that propelled him into the White House as our 9th president.

The Studebakers moved from the mansion shortly after the new century began. Subsequent residents soon found heating and maintaining a structure of such magnitude was fiscally daunting. The Studebaker mansion found itself serving as a headquarters for the American Red Cross, a school for the handicapped, a historical museum, and finally a home for assorted social agencies. Skyrocketing utility and maintenance costs proved too much for these occupants, and by the '70s Tippecanoe's future looked bleak. Local historic preservation groups took up the cause to protect the mansion and restore its status as a working member of the community—notably as South Bend's most lavish and luxurious dining facility.

Ralston Purina's restaurant division bought the mansion in 1979, gave a $3 million interior facelift to the grand lady which originally cost Clement Studebaker $250,000 to build, and opened it as a fine-dining restaurant. Five years later, it was sold to the Japanese-owned Paragon Steakhouse chain, known for its commendable beef and seafood outlets Mountain Jack's and Carvers. It is not surprising that the Tippecanoe Place menu is skewed heavily toward house-specialty prime rib, steaks, and fresh fish, as well as roast duck, rack of lamb, veal tournedos, and elaborate desserts. All of this is prepared and delivered by what must be the most physically fit wait staff in Indiana, judging from the way they bound up and down the stairs to bring food to hungry diners on three, sometimes four levels.

Its upscale 19th century atmosphere has made Tippecanoe Place popular for wedding rehearsal dinners, wedding receptions, and other festive occasions, as well as post-game sustenance and rehashing of yet another titanic struggle of the Notre Dame football team under the shadow of the Golden Dome. It's the kind of culinary setting that has diners believing, "I was meant for this."

COQ AU VIN (serves 2)

1 fresh chicken, boned, split, and cut into 6 pieces: 2 legs, 2 breasts, and 2 thighs
flour enough to dust the chicken parts
3 ounces salad oil
2 teaspoons fresh minced garlic
8 ounces large-diced onion
6 ounces mushrooms, sliced or quartered
12 ounces red wine
8 ounces brown sauce (or any brown gravy, cream of mushroom soup, or lightly thickened beef broth)
salt and white pepper to taste

Cut chicken into pieces. Flour and sauté in salad oil on all sides until golden brown. Remove from pan and keep warm. Add minced garlic and cook for 30 seconds, taking care not to burn. Add diced onions and cook for 5–6 minutes, or until tender but not brown. Add the mushrooms and cook for 2–3 minutes. At this time, remove any excess grease, and add the red wine.

Return chicken pieces to the pan and reduce wine to one-third its volume. Add brown sauce. Bring to a boil, then turn down to a simmer, and cook for 30–40 minutes. Adjust seasoning with salt and pepper.

SOUTHERN PECAN PIE (6–8 servings)

¼ cup butter
1 cup pecan halves or pieces
unbaked 10-inch deep dish pie shell
1 cup brown sugar
1 cup corn syrup
3 eggs
2 teaspoons vanilla

Melt butter. Put nuts in bottom of pie shell. Mix remaining ingredients, including melted butter, well. Pour mixture over the nuts. Bake at 350° for 15 minutes, then reduce oven temperature to 300° and bake an additional 30 minutes, or until it is just set in the center. Cool to room temperature and serve plain or with whipped cream or ice cream.

Welliver's Smorgasbord
HAGERSTOWN

40 E. Main Street (State Road 38)   (765) 489-4131

Open Thursday 4:30–8 P.M., Friday 4:30–9 P.M.,
Saturday 4–9 P.M., Sunday 11 A.M.–8 P.M.

When Elmira, New York native Guy Welliver got out of the Navy
in 1946, he and his new bride Bette settled down in Hagerstown,
near her hometown of Richmond. Guy had intended to open a
men's clothing store, but quickly switched gears upon learning that
a tiny downtown diner called the Hagerstown Grill was for sale.
The Wellivers bought it for a song, and went to considerable lengths
to set it apart by providing hearty buffet lunches and dinners featuring pan-fried chicken, baked and fried fish, roast beef, salads, vegetables, and pies. Indeed, their extensive salad and side dish array is
believed to have first introduced the concept of salad bars to Indiana
citizenry.

The reponse to these daily feastings was so encouraging that
Welliver unleashed an even more elaborate smorgasbord on Sundays. It soon attracted trencherfolk from throughout central Indiana and neighboring Ohio. By 1950, the growing intensity of customer response prompted the Wellivers to throw caution to the winds
and offer their full-blast smorgasbord bounty Thursday through
Sunday at prices that gave patrons change for their five-dollar bill.

The year 1977 produced a turning point for Welliver's—the
debut on the buffet table of peel-and-eat shrimp. This was a fortu-
itous bonus courtesy of the owners of the Tank, the once enor-
mously popular seafood buffet operation in New Castle, fondly
remembered for its five-dollar lobsters in the early '70s. When the
Tank's colorful barn structure burned to the ground, the owners let
Welliver's have their shrimp inventory. Guy deposited a mountain of
peel-and-eaters on the buffet. Such a delicacy on a low-price, all-
you-can-eat basis was a "died and gone to heaven" dining experience, and his customers made it abundantly clear that they expected
the shrimp to continue.

With the weekend buffets and its centerpiece shrimp attraction
increasing the throngs, Welliver and his family were compelled to
expand the restaurant many times over until the 50-seat Hagers-

town Grill blossomed into a dining behemoth with seating for 500. This includes a full-service dining menu featuring hefty steaks, fried chicken, crab legs, and seafood dinners for those daunted by the smorgasbord, with its over 100 items of meats, vegetables, fruits, salads, and desserts. The smorgasbord price tag is now in the $13–$16 range, with pan-fried chicken, roast beef, fried shrimp, chicken livers, smoked sausage, and of course, the steamed shrimp, holding sway.

In January 1999, Guy Welliver, just entering his 9th decade after over half a century of giving customers more than their money's worth in terms of calories, retired, turning the business over to his three daughters, Mary, Janie, and Margaret, and son-in-law Dale Purvis. They are fully up to the task of guiding Welliver's Smorgasbord into the new millennium, so that its long-time fans may continue peeling, eating, and loosening their belts another notch.

WELLIVER'S SMORGASBORD CHEESE BALL

6 pounds cream cheese
1 1/4 pounds crumbled blue cheese
3 tablespoons granulated garlic powder (not garlic salt)

1 teaspoon Worcestershire sauce
1 1/2 tablespoons red hot sauce
chopped pecans for coating

Mix cheeses and seasonings thoroughly and shape into balls or logs of the desired size; then roll in chopped pecans. (The amount of garlic, Worcestershire sauce, or hot sauce may be varied to suit individual taste. Add crumbled blue cheese sparingly to suit taste.)

CREAM OF ONION SOUP (serves 6)

6 tablespoons margarine
4 tablespoons flour
4 cups milk
1/2 cup chicken stock
1 cup chopped onions

1/2 teaspoon salt
1/4 teaspoon pepper
1/4 cup finely cut green onions
1 1/2 cups half and half

Melt 2 tablespoons of margarine in top of double boiler. Add flour and mix well. Add milk and chicken stock. Beat with wire whip to blend together and keep smooth.

Sauté onions in 4 tablespoons of margarine for 3 minutes. Add to soup mixture. Cook for 15 minutes. Add salt, pepper, green onions, and half and half. Mix and serve.

Comfort Foods

More than a few Hoosier dining spots have prospered by catering to Hoosier hunger pangs, with food supplied either cheaply and with dispatch, or else with enough distinction to justify a journey. Behold some of Indiana's most accomplished comfort food specialists. Phone them for hours of operation.

Bay Window
GREENWOOD

202 W. Main Street   (317) 882-1330

Open for lunch Tuesday–Saturday at 11 A.M.

This winsome luncheon tea room in downtown Greenwood was opened in 1983 by Mary Jay and Jennie Plumer. It throve as folks took a shine to their signature chicken and cranberry salad, deli sandwiches on home-baked bread, wide range of soups highlighted by the cream of broccoli, assorted quiches, and the anti-quiche, "The Real Man's Grilled Reuben," plus guilt-infused home-baked pies and cakes. The brother-and-sister team of Marty Armbruster and Jane Kennedy purchased the Bay Window from Mary Jay in 1999, giving us the assurance that its winning formula will remain intact.

Bazbeaux Pizza
INDIANAPOLIS

832 E. Westfield Boulevard   (317) 255-5711

334 Massachusetts Avenue   (317) 636-7662

Open for lunch and dinner daily

Jim Berman opened Bazbeaux Pizza in 1986 next to the fire station in Indianapolis' Broad Ripple neighborhood and proved to Hoosier pizza mavens that there are other toppings besides sausage, pepperoni, and anchovies. From its wooden shack-like structure, Bazbeaux offers Greek pizza, topped with spinach and olives; ham and pineapple–loaded Hawaiian pizza; and pizzas infused with basil, garlic, sun-dried tomatoes—even cheeses that are not mozzarella. These gourmet pizzas are now a part of our culture, but Berman won sufficient acclaim with them to justify opening a downtown outpost on Massachusetts Avenue.

Broad Ripple Brewpub
INDIANAPOLIS

840 E. 65th Street   (317) 253-2739

Open for lunch and dinner daily at 11 A.M.

Britisher John Hill and his wife Nancy blazed the trail for brew pubs in Indiana once the federal government removed the legal shackles that prevented the brewing and serving of homemade suds on the same premises. They opened the Broad Ripple Brewpub about two blocks from their acclaimed Corner Wine Bar in Indianapolis' Broad Ripple neighborhood, as a showcase for Hill's repertoire of ales, porters, stouts, and wheat brews. The dark wood setting oozes with the authenticity of the neighborhood pubs of Hill's native land. Nancy Hill sees to it that the menu marches in step, with such stiff-upper-lip sustenance as shepherd's pie, beer-battered fish and chips, and Scotch eggs (hard-boiled eggs encased in sausage).

Chalkies Restaurant and Billiards

INDIANAPOLIS

5603 E. 82nd Street   (317) 578-2221

Open daily

At Chalkies you can enjoy grilled duck quesadilla, prime rib, dry-aged New York strip, lobster linguine, and shrimp and pasta, with creme brûlée for dessert—before, after, or during a game of pool. Under brothers Marvin, Scott, and Chris McKay, Chalkies in the Castleton area unveils a no-smoking 18-table pool room, large bar area with obligatory big screens to monitor the nation's sporting events, and chef Chris Jones' distinguished menu, which for the nibbler can include barbecued chicken pot stickers, brie cheese wrapped in won ton and seared, shrimp cocktail, and gourmet pizzas. As my stogie-smoking Uncle Louie, a veteran of the Chicago pool hall circuit, might say after getting a load of the pure-aired, aromatic confines of Chalkies, "What's this world coming to?"

Country Cook Inn

GREENTOWN

10531 E. 180 South   (765) 628-7676

Open for lunch Tuesday–Friday, for dinner by reservation Tuesday–Saturday

It was in the fall of 1979 that Gary and Arlene Voorhis combined their interests in the environment and midwestern country cooking to create a passive solar–heated restaurant built into the side of a hill on their farm in Greentown in Howard County. Gary, an engineer by trade, provided the environmentally correct architecture and engineering; Arlene established her equally efficient fixed-price menu, offering two different main courses each night plus salad bar and dessert. Baked cod is a nightly staple; roast beef, baked ham, roast turkey, pork loin, and fried chicken make guest appearances throughout the week. Folks both nearby and far away are accustomed to making frequent pilgrimages to Country Cook Inn to immerse themselves in its unique ambience and comforting menu. It's open for lunch to the general public, but dinner is by reservation only. Be sure to get directions, for it's off the road, deep in the country, with corn and soybeans the only landmarks.

Delafield's
GREENWOOD

50 Airport Parkway   (317) 882-5282

Open for lunch and dinner every day at 11 A.M., and breakfast Sunday at 9 A.M.

Tanis Fields opened this small café in a Greenwood strip center less than a mile west of the Greenwood exit off I-65 in 1996. Word quickly spread, and it became a popular destination for creative deli sandwiches, gourmet coffees, and spectacular homemade pies and cakes as culled from the recipe box of Tanis's late mother, Louise Fields. Of special note are Delafield's chicken salad on puff pastry and the imposing peasant's sandwich, stacked jaw-stretchingly high with ham, salami, pastrami, roast peppers, grilled eggplant, basil, and melted provolone on French bread. That and a hefty piece of coconut cream pie can keep many a Delafield's regular fueled for days.

Edwards Drive-In
INDIANAPOLIS

2126 S. Sherman Drive   (317) 786-1638

Open for lunch and dinner daily

Herb Edwards plunged into the drive-in restaurant experience as a Dog n Suds franchisee in 1957, during the golden era of drive-ins. When Dog n Suds faltered in the early '70s, Edwards attached his own name to his popular southside Indianapolis curb-service eatery, drawing strong support with hand-breaded, fried pork tenderloin and onion rings. After Herb's death in 1976, his son, Tom, took over, and had something of an epiphany when Indiana's fabled blizzard of January 1978 trapped him in the drive-in for three days before his family and—more to the point—customers could reach him. He spent those lonely days drawing up plans for indoor dining. Then in the spring of '78, just as workmen were about to add the indoor dining room, a tornado passing through the southside severely damaged the drive-in, with the adventitious result that a complete makeover was possible. The now full-service, all-weather Edwards Drive-in has indoor seating for 144 and curbside service for those seeking the movable feast of burgers, fries, rings, coney dogs, frosted root beer, and tenderloins. Edwards is currently considered the essence of '50s retro, with Wurlitzer jukeboxes cranking out the tunes of Elvis, Chuck, Fats, and Jerry Lee. Tom's son Jeff and daughter Terri have now joined the effort, propelling the '50s into the '00s.

Frank and Mary's
PITTSBORO

21–25 E. Main Street/State Road 136   (765) 892-3485

Open for lunch and dinner Monday–Saturday at 11 A.M.

Frank and Mary Herring's fame and fortune over the last half of the 20th century has revolved around that whiskered monarch of the mire, the catfish. In 1945, Frank and Mary opened a small tavern in downtown Pittsboro in Hendricks County, west of Indianapolis, serving up sandwiches and Mary's pan-fried cod. In 1951, Frank discovered the joys of fried catfish, long popular in the South but dismissed in the North as a lowlife bottom feeder. Frank felt that the catfish, as plucked specifically from the St. John's River in Florida, was worthy of the Hoosier palate, especially when deep fried in the Herrings' cornmeal batter. Frank and Mary quickly converted the skeptical, drawing SRO crowds on weekends to justify continual expansions of the restaurant. It now seats 300 under the guidance of Frank and Mary's son, Bob, and their grandchildren, Larry, Tom, and Jeff Herring, with Larry's son Alex waiting in the wings. The Herrings rely on a Mississippi catfish farm to provide their star attraction with the consistency and volume their clientele demand. Fried chicken, frog legs, oysters, scallops, and onion rings are also available. Frank and Mary's serves as something of a museum, paying tribute to Pittsboro's favorite son, race driver Jeff Gordon, whose stunning success on the NASCAR circuit was no doubt inspired by the fame of Frank and Mary's catfish.

G.T. South's Rib House
INDIANAPOLIS

5711 E. 71st Street   (317) 849-6997

Open for lunch and dinner Monday–Saturday

When Travis South departed a longtime sales job to open his dream ribbery on the northeastside in 1992, he had zero experience in the restaurant business, but he knew what he liked and that Indy lacked what he liked—true Southern smoked barbecue of the kind that nourished him in his Georgia youth. This involves subjecting assorted pork products, chicken, even turkey, to a hickory wood smoker for a dozen hours or so according to the commandment "Cook it low and smoke it slow." Soon South had to take crash courses in remodeling, compelled to sextuple his seating capacity from its original 30 seats, as customers became enamored of ribs, offered "dry" (without sauce) or "wet" (swab it on), and his "pulled pork" platters, with pork pulled from the shoulder and piled high on plate or bun. All this is rendered amidst a no-frills decor and genuine Southern hospitality delivering a no-nonsense chowdown.

Indianapolis City Market
INDIANAPOLIS

Market & Alabama Streets   (317) 634-9266

Open for breakfast and lunch Monday–Saturday

City Market downtown has been an endearing part of Indianapolis' cultural history since 1886, when it first served as a 19th century supermarket. Farmers set up stands and wagons inside and out to sell the bounty from their fields and their stockyards. This is where people came to buy their fresh meats and produce, and assorted goods and services. The march of time, and the almost bewildering waves of change it afflicts on economic, demographic, and lifestyle trends, has put the venerable City Market on slippery financial footing the last two decades. But she is a stubborn old queen who demands attention and respect, and has evolved into a lunchtime food festival for those who keep the machinery of government, the courts, and law enforcement churning across the street in the City-County building, and anyone else looking for a quick bite and a full dose of history in its three colorful wings. On hand are more than 25 vendors of everything from Mexican, Oriental, Cajun, Greek, and Middle Eastern to Philadelphia cheese steak. Receiving the most reverential treatment are Libby's Deli, a seven-decade purveyor of corned beef, pastrami, and other Jewish delicacies under the tutelage of Libby Fogle; Jumbo's, dispensing hefty roast beef and barbecue pork sandwiches and well-stocked stews and chowders to ward off whatever you want warded off; and Cath, Inc, one of the city's first gourmet coffee outlets, under the inspirational leadership of the late Cathy Peachey. You can still find fresh fruits, imported foods, and even fresh meats and seafood at City Market, as well as get your shoes shined and repaired, your dress hemmed, and your back rubbed. But now its mission for this century is to do lunch, and at some stands breakfast, quickly and on the fly.

Ivanhoe's
UPLAND

398 S. Main Street   (765) 998-7261

Open for lunch and dinner daily

In 1965, Ivan and Carol Slain decided to quit their factory jobs to open a small drive-in in their hometown of Upland in Grant County, between Gas City and Hartford City off State Road 22. With Taylor University just up the road, they felt it would be prudent to offer burgers, fries, tenderloins, onion rings, and other required nutrients of the college student diet, including traditional shakes and sundaes. Then their creative juices kicked in and they started adding new flavors with an escalating number of nutted, candied, and syruped additives, until they came up with 100 different shakes and 100 different sundaes. Customers can study the encyclopedic menu detailing sundaes and shakes called Oreo Mint, Peanut Butter Smash, Strawberry Cookie Banana, and Pineapple Upside Down, with mocha and cappuccino shakes for the terminally trendy and, for the late riser, the breakfast shake featuring bananas and Rice Krispies— all the while lamenting the loss of the jalapeño pepper sundae and dill pickle shake as flavors that were ahead of their time. The Slains' son, Mark, will be put in charge of new flavors for the 21st century.

Jazz Cooker
INDIANAPOLIS

925 E. Westfield Boulevard   (317) 253-2883

Open for lunch and dinner Tuesday–Saturday

In 1986 Lynn Beatty brought the fiery delights of Cajun cuisine to Indianapolis citizens and showed them there was nothing to fear from the bold, spicy flavors of her array of gumbo stews, jambalayas, chicken creoles, blackened redfish and beef, and crawfish étouffé. All of it is concocted and brewed in one of Broad Ripple's oldest structures, a wonderfully creaky two-story white house with an expansive porch for outdoor summer dining and imbibing. On weekends, inside or out, you can groove on the Dick Laswell Trio's hot jazz licks.

Jonathan Byrd's Cafeteria
GREENWOOD

100 Byrd Way   (317) 881-8888

Open daily for lunch and dinner

Jonathan Byrd is a big man who thinks big. The cafeteria he opened in 1988 off the Greenwood exit of I-65 South has dining room seating for 500 and several banquet and meeting rooms to accommodate another 600. Feeding the multitudes in a family dining setting was a longtime dream for the affable Byrd after several years of running Kentucky Fried Chicken franchises with his father. And indeed, chicken is the marquee attraction of Jonathan Byrd's, and bearing more than a passing flavor resemblance to the Colonel's. Vying for equal billing amid the some 200 items on the 88-foot-long serving line are roast beef, baked cod, cheese and macaroni, pork roast and stuffing, and home-baked pies and desserts—strategically placed at the beginning of the line at the point of least resistance. Byrd, known for his involvement in Indy racing as a car owner, provides a comforting all-American ambiance in his dining room, with Norman Rockwell paintings gracing the walls. And for diners loading up their trays, seeing Jonathan Byrd greeting customers can also be comforting, for he cuts an imposing figure that suggests he eats and immensely enjoys his own cooking.

Knobby's Restaurant
INDIANAPOLIS

5201 N. Keystone Avenue   (317) 251-9497

Open for breakfast, lunch, and dinner Monday–Saturday

Knobby's traces its roots back to 1951 as a drive-in opened by William Knoll on 38th Street in the shadow of the Indiana State Fairgrounds. Its success as one of the city's first carhop-serviced drive-ins prompted Knoll to open two more on Keystone and Shadeland avenues on the northeastside. As drive-ins lost their lustre in the '70s, Knoll closed the Shadeland and 38th Street locations, concentrating on the North Keystone outpost, which opened in 1954, and turning it into a full-service restaurant in the '60s, when he first started serving cocktails. There it has persevered under William Knoll's son, Tom, from breakfast through dinner, functioning as your daddy's and granddad's restaurant with an economical mix of Middle America reliables—carved roast beef, chicken-fried steak, veal cutlets, fried chicken and shrimp, and ham steak, free of glitz and flash. Patrons of Fairgrounds events still find Knobby's a reliable luncheon spot, and hordes of loyal customers through the decades have received solid sustenance there at all three meals.

Laughner's Cafeteria
FRANKLIN, PLAINFIELD, AND 4 LOCATIONS IN
INDIANAPOLIS

(317) 783-2907

Open daily for lunch and dinner

Laughner's Cafeteria traces its roots back to 1888, when the Jonathan Laughner family opened a small candy and confectionery store on Indiana Avenue in downtown Indianapolis. As such it ranks as Indiana's longest running dining act. Under the rubric Laughner's Dairy Lunch it soon offered more substantial sustenance, attracting Indy's growing legion of downtown office workers with cheap, quick lunches they could choose themselves from the serving line. The latter half of the 20th century found Laughner's expanding throughout Indianapolis with larger, homier forums and more extensive arrays of salads, vegetables, desserts, and entrées—roast beef, roast turkey, baked fish, the always controversial liver and onions, and fried chicken that was immortalized by Jane and Michael Stern, those intrepid chroniclers of American "real food," in a 1988 *New Yorker* article. With the onset of aggressive competition from casual theme restaurants such as Applebee's and Chili's, Rick and Chip Laughner, representing the 4th generation of the family, have downsized the cafeteria roster in recent years and developed a more varied approach to comfort food, with larger theme restaurants, like the Oven in Avon and Loon Lake Lodge in Castleton, in addition to smaller cafeteria operations.

Lemon Drop
ANDERSON

1701 Mounds Road   (765) 644-9055

Open for lunch and dinner Monday–Saturday

The Lemon Drop was so named not because of the lemon yellow color of the squat stone building that shelters its centerpiece grill and counter and booth-seating for 27, but because the owner's name was Mike Lemon. Mike opened this hamburger stand near

Anderson's General Motors Guide plant in 1954. In 1972, he sold the Lemon Drop to the current owner, Bill Pitts, who laudably resisted the urge to rename it "The Pitts Stop." Pitts carried on the Lemon Drop's legacy of distinctive burgers, notably the cheeseburger on toast and the fabled onion burger, with grilled patties festooned with onions, so that Andersonians you come in contact with later in the day know precisely where you had lunch. Breaded and grilled tenderloins and fried fish round out the hit-the-spot menu. Mr. Pitts is an engaging gentlemen with strong opinions on current affairs, some of which he displays on a marquee outside the restaurant, making a journey to the Lemon Drop an educational as well as a culinary experience.

Louie's Coney Island
KOKOMO

119 E. Sycamore Street   (765) 459-9649

Open for breakfast, lunch, and dinner 8 A.M.–6 P.M.

Louie's Coney Island has been a Kokomo institution since 1943, when Greek-born Louie Volikas and his bride, Sophia, were lured by Louie's father, Gus, from Brooklyn to the Hoosier hinterlands to help his uncle, John Fafalios, with a burgeoning diner business. Fafalios had opened the diner approximately ten years before as the Union Grill on Union Street. With Louie and Sophia's arrival, the diner ultimately found its way to the present 36-seat location on Sycamore Street, where its clientele come to satisfy cravings for coney dogs, burgers, chili, and most of all, bakes—seasoned ground beef rolled into cylindrical shapes and baked in a CIA-caliber secret-recipe tomato sauce, then deposited in hot dog buns, ladled with coney sauce, sprinkled with onions, and labeled a classic by those who indulge. Kokomonians exiled to far-flung lands have been known to have bakes dispatched to them on a regular basis. And under the tutelage of the third generation of Volikases—son Dino and daughter Toula Valikas-Linville—Louie's Coney Island bake has now infiltrated the Chicago market via the Vienna Sausage Company, whose chieftains know a worthy comfort sandwich when they wolf one down.

Mayberry Café
DANVILLE

Main & Jefferson Streets (317) 745-4067

Open for lunch and dinner daily

When Brad and Christine Born bought this breakfast-lunch eatery across from the Hendricks County courthouse in 1989, they operated with the concept and name they inherited—the Main Street Café. After three years of mediocre business, Brad decided to give the café an image makeover. Scrapping breakfast in favor of lunch and dinner, he renamed it the Mayberry Café in tribute to the folks of Mayberry, North Carolina, and adorned it with photos of its most prominent citizens: Sheriff Andy Taylor and son Opie, Aunt Bee, and that towering titan of law enforcement, Deputy Barney Fife, as they appeared for eight seasons and 249 episodes on the *Andy Griffith Show*. Not only did the Borns' business improve, it became a national destination for busloads of Andy Griffith Show fan club members, kneeling and eating at the shrine of their heroes from Gomer to Goober. They come back for the food—such country fixin's as fried chicken, catfish, and steak, as well as baked brie with almonds and shrimp primavera for urban refugees. The Mayberry Café also sells books, videos, and apparel germane to the Andy Griffith tribe, including a few of Aunt Bee's recipe books. For the record, the Borns do not serve, either on the plate or in the Ball jar, Aunt Bee's fabled pickles, with their haunting whiff of kerosene.

MCL Cafeteria
(18 LOCATIONS IN INDIANA)

(317)-257-5425

Open daily for lunch and dinner

The Laughner name is prominent in the launching of Laughner Cafeteria's biggest rival, MCL Cafeterias. For it was a cousin from a different branch of the family, George Laughner, who founded MCL in partnership with Charles McGaughey in 1950. Operating in large, free-standing buildings and select shopping malls, MCL mushroomed into neighboring Illinois and Ohio, and currently has 27 locations, 10 of them in the Indianapolis area. MCL figures it provides 10-million meals a year for those in pursuit of Grandma-influenced fried chicken, turkey and stuffing, roast beef, yeast rolls, and a dizzying array of salads and desserts. As a cafeteria, MCL is particularly appealing to those on a diet, giving them much to choose from to maintain that diet. For that very reason, it is even more appealing to those who are not on a diet but perhaps should be after one lap through the serving line.

Mug 'n Bun Drive-In
SPEEDWAY

5211 W. 10th Street   (317) 244-5669

Open for lunch and dinner daily

In 1960, Morris May used the proceeds of a splendid day at a Las Vegas blackjack table to put a down payment on a FrosTop franchise root beer drive-in at West 10th and Lynhurst Drive in Speedway. The FrosTop had been in operation since 1955, but May expanded its menu, redubbed it the Mug 'n Bun in 1964, and guided it to its current status as Indianapolis' oldest continuing drive-in. Mug 'n Bun became renowned for May's secret-recipe coney sauce, homemade frosted root beer, and fried fish sandwiches—originally available only on meatless Fridays to accommodate his Catholic clientele. A visionary, May was never afraid to augment his traditional drive-in fare of burgers, fries, tenderloins, onion rings, shakes, and malts with such trendy items as fried oysters, catfish, and jalapeño tater tots. Fire damaged the building in the mid-'70s, and May feared he would be out of commission for good. But eight months later he reopened, and when that first day was the busiest ever, May was encouraged to add picnic-table seating, heated to enhance Mug 'n Bun's year-round, all-weather ambience. He and his family also worked hard to make the drive-in a family restaurant, discouraging its use as an *American Graffiti*–type teen hangout. May decided to hang up his apron in 1999, selling Mug 'n Bun to brothers Jay and Ron Watson.

Nick's Chili Parlor
INDIANAPOLIS

2621 Lafayette Road   (317) 924-5005

Open for lunch and dinner Monday–Saturday

Nick Ferris and his father, Jim, were in the wholesale food business when they decided to open a chili outlet in an Indianapolis market that was sorely in need of one in the early '70s. Having no cherished family recipe to turn to, they concocted their own, developed and self-tested it at the North American Food Laboratory in Indianapolis, and started serving it up in 1974 in a former Roy Rogers Roast Beef Restaurant on the city's westside. They succeeded where Roy, Dale, and Trigger could not. Ground beef, red beans, and chili spices with a mild kick proved a winning formula, either in tandem with optional spaghetti, onions, and shredded cheese or lavishly spread over the skillet-grilled hot dogs and Polish sausages on full alert for Indy's longest lasting chili experience.

Nick's English Hut
BLOOMINGTON

423 E. Kirkwood Avenue   (812) 332-4040

Open for lunch and dinner daily

Nick's English Hut is probably the most fabled of Bloomington's and Indiana University's imbibing and nibbling haunts. It dates back to the mid-1920s under the gregarious leadership of Greek-born Nick Hrisomalos, who kept his academic clientele well-fueled with burgers and beer at the small, no-frills establishment with the somewhat dignified stiff-upper-lip moniker. The current owner, Dick Barnes, bought this Kirkwood Avenue institution in 1957, shortly after Nick's death, fully honoring the founder's legacy, while elevating and continually expanding its ambience to wood-beamed pub status, with pool table and dartboard fitness centers, hearty menus revolving around pizzas and strombolis, and brew by the mug, pitcher, or personal pail. Nick's also serves as a clearing house for Indiana University basketball and all stories, discussions, rumors, and celebrations involving Bobby Knight.

Pa & Ma's Barbecue
INDIANAPOLIS
974 W. 27th Street   (317) 924-3698

Open for lunch and dinner Tuesday–Saturday

The granddaddy and grandma of Indianapolis barbecue joints, Pa & Ma's was opened on the westside in 1940 by Rodney and Anna Britt. Shortly afterward, Rodney's cousin, Mary Wilson, joined them. Pa & Ma's has dispensed spareribs, rib tips, and chicken, all cooked directly over charcoal in a large pit just off the front entrance, from a sturdy red brick building on West 27th Street, with the smoke and aromas allowed to waft into the neighborhood. Also a selling point—and, to those wimpy of tastebud, a genuine challenge—has been the uncompromisingly spicy hot barbecue sauce Rodney Britt concocted and Mary Wilson offered as Pa & Ma's only sauce during her four-decade tenure. It gives those ribs and tips a zest and a fiery personality that inspired authors Greg Johnson and Vince Staten to conclude in their 1988 book *Real Barbecue* that Pa & Ma's sauce was the hottest in the land. When Mary Wilson retired in 1983, her successors, the Reverend George Williamson and his family, took mercy on loyal but aging customers whose constitutions could no longer handle the sauce, and gave a choice of "mild" and "sweet" versions as well. In 1996, the Williamsons sold Pa & Ma's to Alisa Langford, who has continued the barbecue tradition and added such soul staples as meat loaf, pigs' feet, pork chops, and greens.

Sahm's Restaurant
FISHERS
11590 Allisonville Road   (317)-842-1577

Open daily for lunch and dinner

Sahm's is a family affair, founded by Ed Sahm in 1986, as something of a casual dining outpost for denizens of Carmel, Noblesville, Castleton, Morse Reservoir, and Fishers, where it is located off 116th and Allisonville Road. While once pretty much by its lonesome, Sahm's now has an ever-growing cadre of dining companions clustered around that intersection, but blithely continues to provide its loyal clientele with wide-ranging, creative takes on cuisine Americana, from power soups, salads, and sandwiches to steaks, swordfish, seafood kebabs and platters, chicken cordon bleu, and several pasta dishes. And the citizens of Fishers, Indiana can give Sahm much of the credit for introducing their town to the populace at large, and bringing in others to share the bounty.

Some Guys Pasta & Pizza Grill
INDIANAPOLIS

6325 N. Allisonville Road   (317)-257-1364

Open for lunch Tuesday–Friday, dinner Tuesday–Sunday

In 1989, Keith and Nancy Carey took over a small strip mall storefront off 62nd and Allisonville Road in Indianapolis that had been home to several pizzerias and elevated it to gourmet pizza status. In choosing a name for their establishment, the Careys were influenced by the "guys" moniker being applied to several East Coast businesses as in "Two Guys Who Are Brothers," "Those Guys," and "Us Guys," so their little pizzeria became "Some Guys," offering some creative pasta dishes and salads and a multitude of zesty pizza offerings, led by the signature mesquite barbecue chicken, with barbecue sauce replacing the traditional tomato. Greece, Jamaica, Thailand, New Mexico, and Melrose, California are also well represented with basil, pesto, olives, shrimp, sun-dried tomatoes, spinach, peanut satay, and such mozzarella alternatives as Gouda, feta, and goat cheese. The traditionalists among their clientele, and there are many, are fully accommodated by two pizzas dubbed "The Classic" and "The Bomb," in which sausage, pepperoni, mushrooms, onions, and mozzarella are prominently featured, with anchovies prepared to make cameo appearances.

Triple XXX Drive-In
WEST LAFAYETTE

2 North Salisbury Street (off State Road 26)
(765) 583-0094

Open 24 hours daily Monday–Saturday, for dinner Sunday

No, this is not the place in West Lafayette to view Russ Meyer and Linda Lovelace film retrospectives. As designated on the bag, "Triple XXX" refers to the high quality of the flour used to pamper the ground sirloin patties that are about to be subjected to the grill. It must make a difference, for its burgers have helped make the Triple XXX Drive-in the state's oldest such dining institution. Perched on an incline of State Road 26 as it heads up to the entrance of Purdue University, it was founded in 1929 by Bert and Katie Wright. Subsequent owners have expanded on the Wrights' concept, making Triple XXX available as a 24-hour treatment facility for sudden munchie attacks. Jack and Ruth Ehresman bought the restaurant in 1980, and, upon their retirement 20 years later, turned it over to their son, Greg and his wife, Carrie. Ehresman touches include grinding fresh sirloin for their floured chopped steak, hand cutting their own breaded pork tenderloins, and concocting their own chili and pork barbecue. Carhop service has given way to indoor seating, and diners can gaze at autographed photos of Purdue football and basketball heroes of yore, many of whom no doubt used the Triple XXX as part of their training table regimen.

Wolf's Bar-B-Que
EVANSVILLE

1414 E. Columbia Street   (812) 423-3599

Open for lunch and dinner daily

Evansvillians are notably fussy about their barbecue, primarily because of the lofty standards set by the Wolf family. These go back to 1927, when Nick Wolf's "everything but the squeal" pork processing and wholesaling business was launched. It provided everything from ribs to chitlins to dog food, and saw to it that area bar patrons had their minimum daily requirement of pickled pigs' feet. In 1954, Nick's sons, Charles and Nicholas II, decided to augment the business with a modest 60-seat nook for barbecued ribs, chicken, and beef, complete with curb service and what is believed to be Indiana's first carry-out window. That original site was expanded to seat 400 in the '80s under a third generation courtesy of Nick II's four children. In the massive dining room, the pork ribs and sliced pork dishes achieve the highest status with their pronounced hickory wood flavor and highly praised catsup-based sauce, known more for its smooth sweetness than for the traditional smoky tang. A 24 by 12-foot pit burns hickory wood 12 hours a day beginning at 5 A.M. to cook the weekly 16,000-pound allotment of pork, beef, chicken, and mutton. Thus Wolf's reputation as Indiana's premier barbecue institution is maintained.

Workingman's Friend
INDIANAPOLIS

234 N. Belmont Street   (317) 636-2067

Open for lunch and dinner

Workingman's Friend began life in 1918 on Indianapolis' near westside as the Belmont Lunch, Louie Stamatkin, proprietor. Recently arrived from Macedonia, Stamatkin set up a short order eatery and bar in a small wooden structure next to the Belmont Railyard. Its workers came there for noontime sustenance and post-work unwinding. It was they who dubbed Louie the "workingman's friend" for allowing them to "do lunch" even when tapped out toward the end of the month, and settling up come payday. When his sons Carl and Earl Stamatkin took over after Louie's death, they rebuilt and expanded the restaurant and renamed it the Workingman's Friend in memory of their father. Under Carl and Earl, the Workingman's Friend became a steak house and a lively night spot in the '40s and '50s, especially when circus trains brought ringmasters, acrobat, clowns, and roustabouts to town. As the railyard faded away, Workingman's Friend has settled in under the direction of Carl's former wife, Mary Gill, and their children Becky and Terry Stamatkin as predominantly a luncheon spot for some of the city's best cheeseburgers, grilled ham and Swiss sandwiches, bean soup, chili, onion rings, and cold beers—a place that is particularly cherished by the doctors of tomorrow who are studying at nearby IU Medical School, and who often choose the Workingman's Friend in ensuing years as the site of their class reunions.

Zydeco's New Orleans Grill
MONROVIA

220 W. Main Street   (317) 996-3900

Open for lunch and dinner, Monday–Saturday

The Morgan County farming community of Monrovia would appear an unlikely place for a genuine New Orleans–style Cajun food forum, but since its inception in late 1998 Zydeco's has been a lively destination restaurant for central Indiana food mavens. It is the handiwork of Debora and Carter Hutchinson, crafted not too long after Hoosier-born Debora met Tulane University graphics design instructor Carter while on one of those travel club junkets to New Orleans. Romance quickly blossomed, and marriage ensued, with Debora luring Carter to her native land to open a restaurant specializing in Louisiana cuisine. They took over an old bar on Monrovia's Main Street, just off State Road 39, and adorned it with streamers, beads, tinsel, and all-season Xmas lights, smacking of Mardi Gras by way of New Year's Eve. Diners are provided with necklaces of plastic pearls to get into the spirit and tap into their libertine side. The menu dwells on home-cooked Cajun cuisine—gumbos, jambalaya, red beans and rice, shrimp Creole, crawfish, and "po' boy" submarine-type sandwiches on French bread. For the most part, Zydeco's does not possess the blowtorch spiciness that Hoosiers expect with Cajun cuisine. But the Hutchinsons provide a vast array of hot sauces to let diners call the shots on temperature control. The more adventurous can nibble deep-fried alligator on a stick. For the record, it tastes like chicken.

Where's the Beef?

Budding restaurateurs in Indiana learned early that longevity in the restaurant business can be greatly enhanced if you can grill a good steak, be it a filet, T-bone, porterhouse, rib-eye, or New York strip. In Indiana, most of the quality chain steakhouses, from such upscale prime beef emporiums as Ruth's Chris, Shula's, Morton's of Chicago, and Sullivans, to moderately priced USDA choice steak forums like Outback, Lone Star, and Mountain Jack's, can usually count on long, productive runs. And independent Hoosier steak grillers, perhaps inspired by their patron, Saint Elmo, have enjoyed a long and prosperous life providing sustenance from the hoof.

Anvil Inn
CICERO

29 E. Jackson Street   (317)-984-4533

Open for dinner, Wednesday–Saturday

At the turn of the 20th century the building that now houses the Anvil Inn in downtown Cicero, off State Road 19 north of Noblesville, created, repaired, and sold quality footwear to horses in the local farming and transportation industries. Thus, when Kathy and Bob Hurst opened their restaurant and bar in 1974, the building's legacy inspired them to name it the Anvil Inn, and decorate its rustic environs with blacksmithian artifacts. The menu follows suit with its muscular country mix of charbroiled filets, porterhouses, and ribeyes, and deep-fried seafood including tilapia, trout, shrimp, and that Hoosier delicacy, catfish. You'll have to look elsewhere for new shoes for your steed, but I'm sure the Dursts can make referrals.

Bobby Joe's Beef and Brew
INDIANAPOLIS

4425 Southport Crossings Road   (317)-882-2333

Open daily for lunch and dinner

The Bobby Joe of Bobby Joe's Beef and Brew off the Southport exit of I-65 South in Indianapolis is the late Bobby Joe Collins, longtime sports reporter, columnist, editor, and resident wit of the *Indianapolis Star*. His colorful, much-honored prose graced the Star for more than four decades. Four years after his 1991 retirement, Collins and his wife, Kristin, opened this rustic restaurant and pub, festooning the premises with photos and memorabilia of Collins's lively newspaper career, extolling the exploits of assorted Hoosier sports legends by the names of A.J., Mario, Oscar, Larry, Slick, Tony, and Bobby, who awarded Collins the ball used in his 500th basketball victory as the hoops guru of Indiana University, which holds a treasured place under glass on the premises. The Beef and Brew menu reflects Collins's belief that thick steaks and stiff drinks are the proper fuel for post-game nourishment and conversation, triggering stories and reminiscences of sports warriors and events of yore, of which Collins was never in short supply. Thus, generous cuts of prime rib, filet, porterhouse, strips, and pork chops dominate the menu, with Kristin getting a word in edgewise with the likes of chicken cordon bleu, coconut shrimp, lobster Newburg, and pasta dishes. Bob Collins lost his longtime battle with cancer shortly after the restaurant opened in 1995, but it serves as a fitting tribute to a gifted writer who lived and chronicled those who lived life at full howl.

Brandywine Steakhouse
GREENFIELD

20 W. Main Street   (317)-462-4466

Open for lunch Monday–Friday; dinner, Monday–Saturday

Loren Cooper first got the folks in James Whitcomb Riley's hometown interested in his charbroiled beef in 1972 in the homey environs of the Brandywine in the heart of downtown Greenfield off U.S. 40. Five years later, he turned the restaurant over to one of his top waitresses, Judy Reimann, who helped turn the Brandywine into a Henry County dining icon as a dependable forum for sustenance from the hoof, augmented by pork chops and fried chicken. Later, she took the bold step of adding seafood to the menu, including lobster, after the practicing beefeaters got word that fish can indeed be prepared in ways beyond the deep fryer that makes it taste good, as opposed to merely good for you. But at the Brandywine Steakhouse, it may take a while for fish to find its way onto the marquee.

Broad Ripple Steakhouse
INDIANAPOLIS

929 E. Westfield Boulevard   (317)-253-8101

Open daily for dinner

Indianapolis dining impresario Hamada Ibrahim, proprietor of the eclectic Midtown Grill and Lulu's, opened this beef emporium in 1987 in a venerable two-story structure on the corner of Winthrop and Westfield in the Broad Ripple neighborhood. Initially it offered moderately priced cuts of choice steaks and chops. But the invasion of such upscale, high-ticket, à la carte chain beef trusts as Ruth's Chris, Sullivan's, Shula's, and Morton's of Chicago prompted the Egyptian-born Ibrahim and his partners to mix it up with the big boys. They gave their dining room a major fashion makeover in 2000 with sleek, contemporary colors and showcased wine rack. The à la carte menu celebrates hefty cuts of prime beef, including bone-in ribeyes, 12-ounce filets, and 22-ounce porterhouses, as well as veal and lamb chops. All of these meats can be adorned with such exotic sauces as cognac peppercorn, morel cream, and mushroom demi-glace. Grilled swordfish, shrimp scampi, sautéd salmon, charbroiled quail, and free-range chicken further enliven the menu. The Broad Ripple Steakhouse offers outdoor patio dining, is joined at the hip with the Outback Bar, and offers a plush cigar-martini emporium on the second floor to further confirm you're living the good life and justifiably so.

Bynum's Steak House
MARTINSVILLE

State Roads 252 & State Road 37   (765) 342-4398

Open for dinner nightly

INDIANAPOLIS

3850 S. Meridian Street   (317) 784-9880

Open for lunch and dinner every day

The father-and-son team of Ed and John Kennedy opened this popular steak place in Martinsville, off State Road 37, in 1983. Here, in a rustic setting, Bynum's lays on belt-loosening cuts of charbroiled steaks. A few years later, Ed and his wife, Lana, opened a second Bynum's on Indianapolis' southside, offering the same heftier-than-thou cuts son John carves up and grills in Martinsville. Pork chops, lamb chops, and chicken also achieve star billing amidst the casual knotty pine decor, in a building guarded by three large plastic heifers that send a strong signal: Bynum's is a place that doesn't deal in sprouts, tofu, and granola.

Fireside South
INDIANAPOLIS

522 E. Raymond Street   (317) 788-4521

Open for lunch and dinner, Monday–Friday

Fireside South traces its roots on Indianapolis' southside to 1935, when the Vehling family established a small neighborhood restaurant in a 19th-century edifice on Raymond Street, across from Garfield Park. In 1947, Ernie and Joan Hohlt purchased the restaurant, and during the next four decades had to expand it several times to accommodate the throngs enamored of their imposing skillet-grilled steaks, prime rib, steak Diane, Swiss steak, and pan-fried round steak. Fireside South also achieved southside acclaim for such delicacies as fried lobster, frog legs, catfish, turtle soup, pickled mushrooms, and salads with hot bacon dressing. With the Hohlts' retirement and passing in the '90s, son Andy Hohlt is guiding the Fireside South into the new millennium, adding a few contemporary touches but seeing to it that steaks retain their star billing.

Haub House
HAUBSTADT

Main Street   (812) 768-6462

Open for dinner Monday–Saturday

Larry Haley built this elaborate and stylish colonial two-story beef and seafood forum in 1970, remodeling a century-old structure that began life as a grain elevator. Its wooden roots are allowed to show in the rear of the building, which also functioned as a general store and as the inimitable Lutz Tavern from Prohibition to shortly before Haley had his way with it through extensive renovation and two expansions. Railroad tracks dominate Main Street in front of the restaurant, harking back to a time when Haubstadt, about 15 miles north of Evansville, was a fairly lively farming and farm product distribution community. Haley chose Haubstadt for his imposing dining spa because he lived two blocks away, and how convenient to be able to invite up to 350 of his closest friends to a dinner of prime steaks, fresh seafood, baby back ribs, prime rib, fried chicken, and pork chops, served in three main dining rooms, with banquet rooms upstairs. Haub House, formerly called Haub's Steak House, also draws folks from nearby Kentucky and Illinois. Haley's son, Kent, and daughter, Diane Dunkel, bring second-generation leadership.

New Ross Steak House
NEW ROSS

Main Street/State Road 136   (765) 723-9291

Open for lunch Monday–Friday, dinner Tuesday–Saturday

This rural steakhouse on State Road 136 southeast of Crawfords-ville achieved icon status under owners Daisy and Jim Stoker who, in 1969, started cooking their choice steak cuts directly on the flat-iron grill, producing filets, strips, rib-eyes, and T-bones with consid-erable sizzling juiciness. Prime rib, catfish, fried chicken, and crab legs have long served in the strong supporting cast. The Stokers retired in 1989, turning the restaurant over to their longtime bar-tender, Joe Johnson, who continues to stoke the Stokers' grill, which seems especially fetching when it's grilling up a dainty 28-ounce T-bone.

Red Dog Steakhouse & Tavern
NORTH SALEM

8 W. Pearl Street   (765) 676-6217

Open for lunch Tuesday–Saturday,
for dinner Monday–Saturday

The Red Dog had long been a shot-and-a-beer forum in the farming community of North Salem in northwest Hendricks County when Don and Peggy Booker took it over in the late '60s to add more solid sustenance, notably in the form of steak. One day, Don took some twigs from an apple tree, set them ablaze under the grate of his brick grill, and commenced to grill T-bones, filets, and rib-eyes with a pleasingly distinctive and pronounced flavor. These applewood-grilled steaks quickly made Red Dog a beef house destination, with some Indianapolis restaurants attempting, but never duplicating, Booker's apple-y touch, mainly because Don wouldn't tell them where he got the wood that produced that unique flavor. Until her retirement in 1996, Peggy continued running the restaurant follow-ing her husband's death in the mid-'80s. Gordon and Sandy Moore now preside over the applewood grill, with their menu also taking in prime rib, pork chops, chicken, and any other meats they can think of that could use an apple a day.

Solly's
REYNOLDS

State Roads 24 & 43   (219) 984-5512

Open for dinner Tuesday–Saturday

Solly's has been staunchly entrenched in the farming community of Reynolds, north of Lafayette, since 1953, for the first 42 years under the gregarious, no-nonsense proprietorship of Burdell Soloman. Solomon cut his own steaks, ground his own hamburger, and presided over the grill, figuring if you want to do things right, you do them yourself. And when he went on vacation, he simply closed the restaurant, figuring customers could wait until he got back. Soloman retired in 1995, and passed away in the fall of 1999. Joe and Donna Mowrer continue his approach and legacy amidst southwestern decor in the dining room and bar, augmenting the menu with broasted chicken and catfish.

Ethnic Eating

There was a time not too long ago when ethnic dining through most of Indiana was confined to Chinese and Italian cuisine. But the '80s produced a young generation of practicing foodies willing to take on reasonably exotic fare from distant lands, infused with spices and seasonings with attitude, even embracing Japanese delicacies once considered unthinkable in mid-America, such as raw fish. Here is a quick tour of ethnic eateries that have made their mark in the midst of the stubborn Midwest traditions of fried foods and grilled red meat.

CHINESE

Chan's Garden
BEECH GROVE

718 Main Street   (317) 784-0862

Open for lunch and dinner Tuesday–Sunday

Wai Ban Chan and his family opened this scarlet-decorated Oriental eatery in downtown Beech Grove in 1970, and soon attracted a very loyal clientele with their signature chicken and vegetable moo goo gai pan; sweet and sour Polynesian duck; and batter-fried, ham-stuffed chicken wings with the lyrical name foong wong gai yick. Chan's Garden seamlessly embraces the spicier and more flavorful Mandarin, Hunan, and Szechwan styles of Chinese cooking to go along with the milder Cantonese style that established Chan's solid reputation.

Forbidden City
INDIANAPOLIS

2605 E. 65th Street (East 65th & Keystone Avenue)
(317) 257-7388

3517 W. 86th Street   (317) 872-2888

Open daily for lunch and dinner

William and Charlotte Hsu's Forbidden City opened in northeast Indianapolis in 1984 with a wide array of creative Mandarin, Hunan, and Szechwan dishes, many of them making their Indiana debut. Standing out are the Mongolian barbecue mix of sliced marinated beef, lamb, and pork tenderloin in spiced sauce; well-seasoned deep fried yellowfish; and Gulf shrimp marinated in white wine. Forbidden City is the only Chinese restaurant where you can order Peking duck on demand, instead of with the customary one day's notice. The Hsus opened a second Forbidden City near West 86th and Michigan Road on the northwest side, and the city's most elaborate Chinese buffet in Castleton (3938 E. 82nd Street; [317] 845-8999). The buffet has been the most visible trend on the Oriental dining scene, allowing diners to sample a wide range of entrées they have been curious about. But it's a trend devotees of the Chinese dining experience deplore, out of concern that it will lead to bland volume preparation common to many cafeterias and undercut the camaraderie of sharing dishes among friends. On the other hand, buffets should eliminate the problem of being hungry an hour later.

Hong Kong Inn
INDIANAPOLIS

8079 E. 38th Street   (317) 898-0613

Open daily for lunch and dinner

The late Jimmy Chung opened the Hong Kong Inn in a shopping

strip off East 38th and Franklin Road in 1969. With his son, Shuiman, at the helm, it now stands as the longest-running Oriental dining attraction in Indianapolis. Through the years, Hong Kong Inn has prospered with its ample assortment of Cantonese, Szechwan, and Mandarin dishes, notably the moo goo gai pan; the Hong Kong wor ba (chopped meats and vegetables in oyster sauce); and its Hong Kong sirloin, sliced and covered with mildly sauced vegetables. Hong Kong Inn was among the last Indianapolis Chinese restaurants to offer an American-style menu, as many felt compelled to do through the '50s and '60s, to accommodate the intractable meat-and-potato member of the family.

Yen Ching
INDIANAPOLIS

8512 E. Washington Street   (317) 899-3270

Open for lunch and dinner Tuesday–Sunday

9150 N. Michigan Road   (317) 228-0868

Open for lunch and dinner daily

Carmel/2332 E. 116th Street   (317) 228-0868

Open for lunch and dinner daily

Yen Ching is a production of seven brothers and sisters of the Ting family (Robert, Lewis, James, Albert, Douglas, Angie, and May), who descended upon Indianapolis in 1981 to introduce spicy and richly flavored Szechwan, Hunan, and Mandarin dishes to a city accustomed to the milder sentiments of Cantonese cooking. Operating from an unpretentious restaurant on the city's far eastside, Yen Ching quickly won converts with its sweet and peppery garlic-sauced house beef; peanut-festooned kung pao chicken, beef, and shrimp dishes; the deep-fried General Zoal's chicken; and arguably the most enchanting hot and sour soup in the metroplex. Recently the Tings added two new restaurants to their kingdom among their most intense northside constituency—off West 86th and Michigan Road, and at 116th and Keystone in Carmel—in keeping with what many consider the area's consistently best Oriental eatery.

ETHIOPIAN

Queen of Sheba
INDIANAPOLIS

936 Indiana Avenue   (317) 638-8426

Open for lunch and dinner daily

Abeda Tesfatsion and her husband, Semeret Chernet, introduced Indianapolis to the interesting dining traditions of their native Ethiopia. At Queen of Sheba, their small, colorfully decorated restaurant on Indiana Avenue directly north of the IUPUI campus, they invite, say, a party of four to sit on low stools at a basket-reed table and partake of dinner from a large communal platter. The utensils consist of large, moist crèpes called enjera, with the diner tearing off a chunk, folding it over, and using it to scoop up an array of spicy dips, meats (well-seasoned lamb, ground beef, chicken), vegetables, lentils, cheeses, and even hard-boiled egg. The conversation-piece combination plates produce the most variety.

GERMAN

Rathskeller
INDIANAPOLIS

Athenaeum
401 E. Michigan Street   (317) 636-0396

Open for lunch Monday–Friday, dinner Tuesday–Saturday

The Rathskeller is ensconced in the lower level of the historic Athenaeum, the social center and legacy of German culture in Indianapolis. As a purveyor of hearty German cuisine, the Rathskeller was an on-again, off-again proposition throughout the '60s and '70s. Then chef Frank Mueller established the culinary consistency it was desperately seeking with his roast beef, rouladen, and sauerbraten, smoked pork chops, Wienerschnitzel, and German sausages. His successors have expanded the menu with fresh seafood and beef dishes. The bar offers a wide range of imported German beers on tap. A lively outdoor Biergarten is open during the summer.

GREEK—MIDDLE EASTERN

Hellas Cafe
INDIANAPOLIS

8501 Westfield Boulevard   (317) 257-6211

Open for lunch and dinner Monday–Saturday, for dinner Sunday at 4 P.M.

In 1986, Alex Koudouris took over a former donut shop off East 86th and Westfield Boulevard in northeast Indianapolis and soon unveiled one of the city's longest-run Greek dining productions with its eggplant and ground beef staple, moussaka; beef and rice-crammed grape leaves, dolmathes; spinach and feta cheese pie, spanakopita; and Hellas' signature dish, chicken oregano. Kathy and Kostas Protopapadakis took over in 1992 for seven productive years before selling to brothers Elias and Anastasios Tsatsakis and their sister Sophia Karnezis in 1999. Their mother, Rubini, stays on hand for quality control. And like any authentic Greek restaurant, Hellas has belly dancers performing on the weekends for post-meal aerobics.

Kabul
INDIANAPOLIS

8553 Ditch Road   (317) 257-1213

Open for dinner Monday–Saturday

Nasir Ayoubi and his family initially opened Kabul in 1985 off the southwest corner of Indianapolis' bustling West 86th and Ditch Road intersection, introducing the cuisine of their native Afghanistan to the Hoosier palate. A few years later, Kabul moved to more spacious and brighter digs in the southeast quadrant of 86th and Ditch, showcasing rice dishes, yogurt marinades, and such mild, flavorful spices as cloves, cinnamon, cumin, and coriander, as applied to lamb, Cornish hen, and vegetables on the spit; the steamed ground beef–filled dumplings called manto; and cabbage leaves stuffed with seasoned beef and rice, dolmathes.

Korey's
INDIANAPOLIS

1850 E. 62nd Street   (317) 251-2252

Open lunch and dinner Monday–Saturday, for dinner Sunday

Bethlehem-born Alex Khoury nearly threw in the towel a year after he opened his small Middle Eastern restaurant and grocery at 62nd and Keystone in Indianapolis in 1981. It seemed folks were judging Korey's by its cover—it still sported the dairy-bar architecture of a failed ice cream shop. But once word got out that Korey's probably had the best lamb and beef gyros in the area, the restaurant caught on, allowing Khoury and his successor in 1990, Issam Mustaklem, to expand the menu to such traditional Greek–Middle Eastern fare as moussaka, spanakopita, kibbeh, and that wondrously intense Greek pastry, baklava.

Parthenon
INDIANAPOLIS

6319 N. Guilford Street   (317) 251-3138

Open for lunch and dinner daily

In light of its 1978 opening in the heart of Broad Ripple, Parthenon is the granddaddy of Middle Eastern–Greek restaurants in Indiana, with Mustafa and Carol Abu-Rumman expanding on the traditional dishes with the likes of chicken oregano, leg of lamb fricassee, prawns topped with bacon and cheese in Florentine sauce, and beef stew seasoned with Greek spices. Among its more notable pastry desserts is strudel stuffed with sweet cheese and ground walnuts topped with syrup, followed on the weekends by belly dancers to demonstrate the best way to keep it from showing.

IRISH

Irish Lion
BLOOMINGTON

212 W. Kirkwood Avenue   (812) 336-9076

Open for lunch and dinner daily

Larry McConnaughy and his wife, Hilda, combined their passions for good food and antiques when they opened the Irish Lion in downtown Bloomington in 1982 in a building on Kirkwood Avenue that traces its ancestry back to 1882. They transformed the structure into an Irish watering and dining mecca that would bring a tear to the eye of any son of the sod, what with Guinness on tap, corned beef and cabbage, Celtic lamb stew, leg of lamb, mutton pie, Irish soda bread, and Baileys Irish Cream mousse on the menu. Chef Mark Hennessy also offers a full range of steaks, prime rib and seafood to show that the Irish can do much more on the sustenance front than merely satisfy your thirst. The McConnaughys operated the continental Magic Horn restaurant in Bloomington for 9 years prior to opening the Irish Lion. They have been in the antiques business since the '60s, and have put the fruits of their labors into the decor, including the 16-foot-long 1860 bar adorned with animal heads that was rescued from a Vincennes saloon. The Irish Lion is also into physical fitness—the restrooms are 22 steep steps up to the second floor, past the banquet rooms.

MEXICAN

El Sol de Tala
INDIANAPOLIS

2444 E. Washington Street   (317) 635-8252

Open for lunch and dinner daily

Maria Taylor, an accomplished chef Mexicana, opened El Sol de Tala as a modest Mexican restaurant and grocery on Indianapolis' near eastside in 1978 in a turn-of-the-century building that was once a theater. A year later, she sold it to its current hard-charging owner, Mexican-born Javier Amezcua, who ultimately jettisoned the grocery and built the restaurant as a bastion for South of the Border cuisine. His expansive menu highlights chiles rellenos (deep-fried poblano peppers stuffed with chihuahua cheese); pork tamales; marinated shredded beef-filled tacos, burritos, and enchiladas; boiled chicken in mole sauce; and a trio of egg dishes featuring Javier's zestier-than-thou salsa and Mexican sausage. In 1999, Amezcua expanded El Sol threefold with mezzanine seating ringing the main dining room and weekend strolling mariachi band concerts.

INDIAN

India Garden
INDIANAPOLIS

830 Broad Ripple Avenue   (317) 253-6060

Open for lunch, Monday–Saturday, for dinner every night

143 N. Illinois Street   (317) 634-6060

Open for lunch and dinner Monday–Saturday

India Garden is the dean of Indianapolis' small colony of Indian restaurants, first opening in 1990 in the heart of Indianapolis' Broad Ripple Avenue, then unveiling a classier rendition downtown in

1999. Under the guidance of owner Jaswant Gidda, India Garden has a wide range of spicy curry and vindaloo sauces as applied to chicken, lamb, shrimp and vegetables, and has clay tandoori ovens to roast yogurt-marinated skinless chicken, marinated shrimp and fish, and lamb kabobs.

India Palace
INDIANAPOLIS

4213 Lafayette Road   (317) 298-0773

Open for lunch and dinner daily

India Palace opened in 1994 in a small strip center directly north of Lafayette Square on Indianapolis' westside, producing some of the more photogenic ethnic dishes in the city in the form of its colorful tandoori chicken and shrimp, glowing with a reddish hue from the marinades. The menu unreels an extensive array of lamb, chicken, shrimp, and vegetarian dishes in well-spiced sauces of escalating temperatures, with the curry and vindaloo sauces commanding the most attention. All of this has allowed India Palace to persevere from a slow start in its somewhat hidden location, with owner Suthminder Pandher able to double the size of the original 60-seat eatery in 1999.

JAPANESE

Daruma
INDIANAPOLIS

3508 W. 86th Street   (317) 875-9727

Open for lunch, Monday–Friday, dinner Monday–Saturday

Daruma is Indiana's oldest continuing Japanese restaurant, starting with a nine-year run on the city's eastside before Tomino Ri Okugawa and Sachiko Weiss moved it to its more visible location at 86th and Michigan Road on the northwestside in 1986. Along with traditional favorites like beef teriyaki and shrimp tempura, it was the first to introduce the colorful spectrum of sushi. Daruma's main dining room gives the appearance of traditional Japanese family dining, with shoes removed while sitting on the floor at tables just a foot off the ground. However, for American patrons who find all this downright awkward and physically uncomfortable, there are wells under the table so that they may dangle their feet.

Sakura
INDIANAPOLIS

7201 N. Keystone Avenue   (317) 259-4171

Open for lunch and dinner Tuesday–Saturday, for dinner Sunday

Sakura Ocean Grill
INDIANAPOLIS

1206 W. 86th Street   (317) 848-8901

Open for lunch and dinner Monday–Saturday, for dinner Sunday

Owned by a family with successful Japanese restaurants in Chicago, Sakura did not introduce sushi to Indianapolis when it opened in its cozy white starter home at 71st and Keystone, but it is where these fresh fish and rice combinations were embraced in a community that once shunned raw fish with the belief, "IT'S ALIVE!!!!" The expertly crafted sushi rolls and the freshness of such sushi headliners as tuna, salmon, squid, octopus, and roe have converted many a wary Hoosier diner into an addict. There was an onrush of commendable sushi palaces in Central Indiana, notably West Lafayette, with the opening of the Isuzu automobile plant. Sakura also offers a wide-ranging menu of Japanese noodle dishes and Korean dishes. And those who want to try it at home can purchase sushi-grade seafood at Sakura's fish mart, just around the corner on 71st Street.

This is what prompted the opening of Sakura Ocean Grill off West 86th and Ditch Road on the northwestside, with a more spacious and attractive dining room and sushi bar and an expansive menu of fresh grilled seafood.

Ginza Japanese Steak House
INDIANAPOLIS

5380 W. 38th Street   (317) 298-3838

Open for lunch and dinner daily

Ginza was originally built in the early 1990s on Indianapolis' westside as your basic slice-and-dice Japanese steakhouse, with the chef cutting up and grilling your meat for you with great flair and knife-wielding showmanship. But gradually it has achieved greater renown for the quality, range, and creative construction of its sushi under the innovative artistry of a maestro named Dagusan. There are creatures who thought they were exempt from the sushi food chain, like sea urchins and baby seahorse, and sushi platters as beautiful as anything in an art gallery.

Mikado
INDIANAPOLIS

148 S. Illinois St.   (317) 972-4180

BLOOMINGTON

895 S. College Mall Road   (812) 333-1950

Open for lunch and dinner daily

Sisters Juping Chi and Yumei Li brought the Japanese dining experience to downtown Indianapolis in 1998 with the city's most attractive Japanese restaurant, across from Circle Centre shopping mall. In addition to its extensive sushi selections, Mikado stresses its fresh peppered seafood dishes, Japanese noodle ensembles, and

Japanese dinner pots of salmon, beef, and vegetables, prepared tableside in flavorful boiling broths. The Mikado in Bloomington opened in1994 in Jackson Creek, a strip center just beyond College Mall, with full sushi bar along with shrimp and seafood tempura and Black Angus beef teriyaki.

KOREAN

Bando
INDIANAPOLIS

8015 Pendleton Pike   (317) 897-8277

Open for lunch and dinner daily

Ma Ma's Restaurant
INDIANAPOLIS

8867 Pendleton Pike   (317) 897-0808

Open for lunch and dinner daily

Korean-born Insuk Terao opened Ma Ma's Restaurant on Pendleton Pike in northeast Indianapolis in 1989, originally calling it Ma Ma's House in deference to the lady presiding over her Korean kitchen—her mother, Im Choe. A year later, Terao sold the restaurant to her assistant chef, Su Lim Yi and moved up the street in pursuit of better parking facilities and a more contemporary look, in opening Bando. Both restaurants have the traditional marinated beef, bulgogi; the sweet-flavored marinated beef short ribs, bulgalbi; the spicy pickled cabbage, kim chee; the sushi-like rice balls, kimbop; and sumptuous meal-in-themselves seafood soups. The meals are accompanied by dazzling array of side nibbles, each item on its own plate, resulting in over 40 plates for a party of four, to the delight of everyone but the dishwasher. Late in 1990, Bando added a sushi bar and Korean barbecue grills for the tableside grilling of meats and fish in the interactive Korean tradition.

RUSSIAN

Russia House Restaurant
INDIANAPOLIS

1475 W. 86th Street   (317) 876-7990

Open for dinner Monday–Saturday

Husband and wife Michael Vladimirov and Tatiana Pali came to this country from their native Moscow in 1992 as ballet dancers, with Ms. Pali a most prominent performer for the Indianapolis Ballet Theatre. They opened Russia House restaurant on Indianapolis' northwest side in 1996, off the southwest corner of West 86th Street and Ditch Road, focusing on Russian home-style cooking. They are best known for their chicken Kiev; beef Stroganoff; borscht; and the meat or cheese-filled dumplings called vareniki. At this time, this is Central Indiana's sole purveyor of Russian cuisine —hearty fare that keeps you light on your feet.

THAI

BANGKOK RESTAURANT
FISHERS

116th & Allisonville Road   (317) 578-1917

Open daily for lunch and dinner

In 1985, the late Sam Balasiri and his wife, Jarunee, unveiled the Thai experience in the Hoosier landscape from their combination restaurant-grocery on Indianapolis' eastside. They soon scrapped the grocery and expanded the restaurant to accommodate enthusiastic customers for Bangkok's combustably spicy soups, pan-fried rice dishes, curry and peanut sauces and sautés, and well-seasoned and spiced chicken, beef, seafood, and pork dishes. In 1990, the Bangkok moved to plusher environs at the Norgate Shopping Plaza off 75th and Keystone; then, as the shopping complex declined, it found its way to its current location at 116th and Allisonville in Fishers.

Destined to Stand the Test of Time

Indiana's hyperactive dining scene of the final two decades of the 20th century produced many distinctive restaurants that seemed destined for productive runs into the 21st.

Adam's Rib & Seafood House
ZIONSVILLE

40 S. Main Street   (317) 873-3301

Open for lunch and dinner Tuesday–Saturday

Jim and Alice Adams helped launch the village of Zionsville's reputation as a quaint restaurant mecca when they opened their beef and seafood emporium in 1973 in an 1860s-vintage structure on brick-paved Main Street. First known for its trencherman cuts of prime rib, the restaurant soon earned equal praise for its seafood, notably the charbroiled yellowfin tuna and halibut, sautéed scallops, crab legs, and frog legs. Adam's Rib also became a haven for the adventurous diner: Adam's jungle and backwoods appetizers feature creatures long believed exempt from the American food chain, such as rattlesnake, camel, giraffe, and hippopotamus. In recent years, they have limited exotic entrées to customer favorites: roast lion, African antelope, black bear, and deep-fried alligator, which tastes like chicken.

Agio
INDIANAPOLIS

635 Massachusetts Avenue   (317) 488-0359

Open for dinner, Tuesday–Sunday

Agio is one of many European-style bistros that opened in the Indianapolis environs during the '90s where distinctive, reasonably priced continental cuisine in a casual setting may be found. With the 1999 opening of their high-ceilinged, southwestern-hued venue in the artsy-funksy, newly gentrified Massachusetts Avenue area of downtown, owners Fred Cooney and Michael Campo give Agio an Italian accent with its array of pastas, grilled meats, and fish. The menu is highlighted by risotto dishes, eggplant lasagna, veal scaloppine, grilled free-range chicken, rack of lamb, and filet mignon glazed with balsamic and black malt vinegars. The dining room and bar display wire sculptures and paintings from local artists, including Mr. Cooney, and are available for purchase right after dessert.

Amalfi Ristorante
INDIANAPOLIS

1351 W. 86th Street   (317) 253-4034

Open for lunch and dinner Monday–Saturday

Arturo Di Rosa opened his cozy Italian bistro in the early '90s. It's a bit hidden from view off the southeast corner of the bustling West 86th & Ditch Road intersection on Indianapolis' northwestside. But devoted customers willingly seek it out in pursuit of Amalfi's critically praised veal dishes, creative pasta ensembles, and the Old World touch brought by Di Rosa's mother, Giuseppina, who gave her recipe box a workout and contributed her signature dry sausage and potato dumpling crammed with tomato and mozzarella. Amalfi's "mother-knows-best" philosophy consistently put it in the Top 5 on assorted Best Indy Restaurants lists through the '90s.

Amici's Ristorante
INDIANPOLIS

601 E. New York Street   (317) 634-0440

Open for dinner Tuesday to Sunday

Amici's had quite an odyssey before it settled comfortably into its current location, a ramshackle wooden two-story house, built around 1867 and looking every bit its age. Josie and Hank Bayt launched the restaurant in 1985 in the old Farmer's Market at East and South streets on the southern edge of downtown. There they were building a solid word-of-mouth following for their bold, creative takes on traditional Italian dishes when, two years later, the Market was closed and torn down, forcing them to move. After a stint on the southside, Amici's moved again in 1989, to New York Street in the historic Lockerbie Square area. It draws heavily from that neighborhood, impressing the clientele with such celebrated specialties as linguine with chicken livers and marinara sauce; fettuccine in a potent gorgonzola sauce; pizzas and calzones; and the explosive shrimp Diavolo, with shrimp, pasta, and broccoli. In 1998, the Bayts opened a similar restaurant in Bloomington called Flora (620 W. 5th Street, [812] 339-8430).

Ambrosia
INDIANAPOLIS

915 Westfield Boulevard   (317) 255-3096

Open for dinner every night

With the opening of Ambrosia in 1980, owner Gino Pizzi introduced northern Italian cuisine, with its emphasis on wine and cream sauces, to central Indiana, and helped give Broad Ripple its reputation for ethnic restaurants. Pizzi, with the help of his Italian-born parents, also triggered an explosion of trendy northern Italian eateries throughout the city in the '80s and '90s that elevated its dining scene considerably. Popular are the veal scaloppine Calvados, sautéed in butter, cream, and brandy, and the lemony veal piccata. Also highly prized by regulars are the sautéed beef tenderloin in mushroom wine sauce, chicken Valdostana (chicken breast infused with prosciutto and fontina in white wine sauce), and numerous pasta dishes with endless permutations on seafood, herbs, vegetables, and sauces. Spawned from Ambrosia in recent years by Pizzi are two similar Italian bistros, Sangiovese (4119 E. 82nd St., [317] 596-0731) in the Clearwater area of northeast Indianapolis and Mangia! (116th and Keystone Avenue, [317] 255-3096) in Carmel.

Arturo's
INDIANAPOLIS

2727 E. 86th Street   (317) 257-4806

Open for lunch, Monday–Friday, and dinner every night

Arturo Di Rosa gave his name to this upscale restaurant off East 86th and Keystone Avenue in northeast Indianapolis when he and business partners opened Arturo's Ristorante in the early '90s. The name stayed when Di Rosa left a year and a half later to open his acclaimed Amalfi's, a few blocks to the west. Chef-owner Patrick Aasen has maintained Arturo's classy culinary reputation and its dimly lit romantic ambience. The delicately sauced pasta and veal dishes have consistently earned kudos, as have such inspirations as peppercorn beef tenderloin in red wine–mustard sauce, poached salmon, and sea bass with tomatoes, garlic, and black olives. Aasen also is known for his Chef's Table, at which select diners enjoy a multi-course meal in the cozy kitchen while they watch a culinary magician at work.

Bonge's Tavern
PERKINSVILLE

9830 W. 280 North, off State Road 13   (765) 734-1625

Open for dinner Tuesday–Saturday

Bonge's Tavern began life in 1847 as a general store in downtown Perkinsville off State Road 13, just north of Lapel. In 1944, Charles Bonge turned it into a watering hole with a menu of bar munchies ranging from hard-boiled eggs to beef jerky to pickled pigs' feet, all available straight from the jar. Mr. Bonge ran his tavern with little fanfare for the next 46 years, with no immediate successors after 1990. Seven years later, Don Kroger purchased the tavern, remodeling the wooden structure but maintaining its historic charm. Recruiting chef Tony Huelster, fresh from star turns at the Glass Chimney in Carmel and Foxfires in Muncie, he turned Bonge's into a casual, funky gourmet restaurant with ever-changing, seasonally adjusted American regional cuisine. The menu is printed on a chalk board over the bar, just below the mounted trophy trout with the obligatory Twinkie in its mouth. On a given night, it might include catfish coated in hash brown potatoes; roast duck in honey apple–thyme sauce; rack of lamb; roast venison; and sea bass. Diners can always count on the Perkinsville Pork, a lengthy pork tenderloin, dipped in flour and egg and coated in Parmesan cheese. It is marvels like these, combined with very limited, no-reservation seating, that makes Bonge's Tavern perhaps the only place in Indiana where diners tailgate in the parking lot, awaiting their table.

Carnegie's
GREENFIELD

100 W. North St.   (317) 462-8480

Open for lunch and dinner Tuesday–Saturday

This is Carnegie as in fabled industrialist Andrew Carnegie. The sturdy, two-story Carnegie Library he provided to serve Greenfield's bookish needs for most of the 20th century is a block north of the Henry County courthouse. And this is where chef Ian Harrison and his partner, Jody Thomson, located their casual fine-dine restaurant early in 1999. After a lengthy tenure at the late, great Benvenuti in downtown Indianapolis, Harrison now lures his loyal clientele to Greenfield for menus that change monthly to take advantage of in-season ingredients and produce and bring about creative takes on roast duck, beef tenderloin, fresh seafood, penne pasta, and steak au poivre in a mushroom brandy sauce. Definitely food for thought.

Central House
NAPOLEON

3684 State Road 229, off State Road 421   (812) 852-2354

Open for dinner Tuesday–Sunday, including Sunday brunch

The building that shelters the gourmet productions of the Central House in Napoleon, 12 miles south of Greensburg, has staunchly withstood the Hoosier elements since 1823. Its roots are infused in the culinary arts; as one of a number of drovers' inns, it originally provided sustenance and accommodations for farmers driving their cattle, pigs, and turkeys to market. In subsequent years, it proved its versatility as a hotel, boarding house, and apartments. A consortium saved and renovated the somewhat creaky structure in the '70s. More recently Marion Waechter rented it, recruiting a capable staff to help turn the Central House into a casual, reasonably priced fine-dining restaurant. Customers have been bedazzled by the artistic plate presentations and by house specialties such as lentil soup; mashed potatoes; veal rolled with prosciutto, provolone, mushrooms, and spinach; braised lamb shank; stuffed pork loin; and fresh seafood. In other words, this old drovers' inn has been reinvigorated for another lengthy run in still another century.

Classic Kitchen
NOBLESVILLE

610 Hannibal Street   (317) 773-7385

Open for lunch Tuesday–Saturday, for dinner Friday–Saturday

World traveler Steven Keneipp opened this distinctive luncheon spot in 1980 with Accent gift shop entrepreneurs Dick and Jane Bridgens in a downtown Noblesville neighborhood as a forum for his rich culinary imagination. His trips down the Nile and the Amazon and journeys up and down prominent mountain ranges have inspired exotic soups, salads, quiches, and pâtés for luncheon through the week in a tea room setting, as well as creative, ever-changing dinner entrées on Friday and Saturday. Thus you may delicately slurp Haitian pumpkin soup from his repertoire of over 250 soup recipes, or commune with salmon baked in foiled pouch; Star of India chicken, seasoned with currants and saffron; or any of several rotating fresh fish and veal dishes. Classic Kitchen is notorious for its desserts, notably Keneipp's unconscionable caramel and chocolate gnocchi.

Corner Wine Bar
INDIANAPOLIS

6331 N. Guilford Avenue   (317) 255-5159

Open for lunch and dinner Monday–Saturday

John and Nancy Hill imported and injected a healthy dose of the Mother Country into this cozy restaurant and pub at the prime corner of Guilford and Westfield Boulevard in Indianapolis' Broad Ripple neighborhood in 1982. The British-born John Hill provides a well-stocked wine cellar and scores of imported beers, most bearing an English accent, while Nancy, his bride from the colonies, lays on such toothsome delicacies as beef tenderloin, chicken breasts in a honey-lime sauce, and Chilean sea bass. Joined at the hip is the Hills' dead ringer of a British neighborhood pub, the Wellington. The Corner Wine Bar features outside dining in the summer. In the winter, there are special four-course dinners, periodic beer and wine tastings, and intensely competitive darts tournaments. For the record, John Hill introduced the brew pub concept to Indiana, with his Broad Ripple Brew Pub two blocks to the northeast.

Different Drummer
WALDEN INN, GREENCASTLE

East Seminary & Vine Streets   (765) 653-2761

Open daily for breakfast, lunch, and dinner

When a group of investors opened the Walden Inn in 1986 as a small hotel and conference center to serve the visitor lodging and entertaining needs of neighboring DePauw University, they recruited Irish-born chef Matthew O'Neill, well known in Indianapolis, to run its restaurant, the Different Drummer, and preside as innkeeper in the contemplative setting inspired by philosopher Henry David Thoreau of Walden Pond. Shortly after arriving, O'Neill had to work through the tragedy of losing his wife, Karen, and an infant son in an automobile accident. Through it all, however, he quickly elevated the Walden Inn and the Different Drummer to premier status with his creative regional American menu featuring delicately sauced fresh fish, sautéed veal and lamb, grilled duck, pan-fried catfish, steaks, and prime rib. The early American decor gives truth to a Thoreau reflection that mirrors the O'Neill approach: "The finest qualities of our nature, like the bloom on fruits, can be preserved only by the most delicate handling."

Dunaway's Palazzo Ossigeno
INDIANAPOLIS

351 S. East Street   (317) 638-7663

Open for lunch and dinner daily

Dunaway's Palazzo Ossigeno, at the edge of Fletcher Place historic neighborhood, is in the former headquarters building of the Indiana Oxygen Company. The old building was lugged five blocks to that location to spare it from the wrecker's ball. Jeff Dunaway, freshly departed from St. Elmo Steak House, bought it, built a two-story addition to accommodate a kitchen and additional dining rooms, and opened in 1999 as an upscale, high-tariff, Italian-accented eatery, augmented by prime steaks in keeping with his St. Elmonian roots. Dunaway recruited chef Tim Brater from Ruth's Chris Steak House to unleash such dishes as spicy-sauced shrimp and linguine Fra Diavolo; herb-crusted chicken, roast pork loin, and duck; and veal chops with prosciutto and fontina. As of this writing, Dunaway's is the lone Indianapolis restaurant with rooftop outdoor dining, giving a splendid view of the downtown skyline to the southeast. It is a particularly lively place on the evening of July Fourth.

Eagle's Nest
INDIANAPOLIS

Hyatt-Regency Hotel
1 South Capitol Avenue   (317) 231-7566

Open for lunch Monday–Friday, for dinner Monday–Sunday

The Eagle's Nest is the upscale restaurant of the downtown Hyatt Regency Hotel. Perched on the 22nd and final floor, it sports a starry, intergalactic ambience and a menu showcasing prime rib, steaks, roast duck, pork tenderloin, veal chops, and fresh seafood. But for many, the Eagle's Nest's most salient feature is the fact that it is the state's only revolving restaurant, slowly giving the diner a 360-degree perspective of the work in progress that is downtown Indianapolis.

Fiddlers Three
SHELBYVILLE

1415 E. Michigan Road   (317) 392-4371

Open for dinner Tuesday–Saturday

In 1971, William and Jenny Dugan took over a Gulf gas station property on Michigan Road in Shelbyville, built a three-level restaurant, dubbed it Fiddlers Three, and prospered as *the* place in Shelbyville for a solid, reliable beef and/or seafood dinner. Fiddlers Three has earned particularly high marks for its prime rib, filets, pork filets, barbecued ribs, and fresh seafood. In 1990, the second-generation contingent, consisting of James Dugan and Kathy and Jay DeMoss—son, daughter, and son-in-law respectively—took over Fiddlers Three as their parents glided into the quality-control consultant phase of semi-retirement.

Fletcher's of Atlanta
ATLANTA

185 W. Main Street   (765) 292-2777

Open Tuesday–Saturday from 5 P.M.

After a memorable run in the mid-'80s with Fletcher's American

Grill and Café in downtown Indianapolis, Fletcher Boyd and his wife, Gloria, decided they needed some fresh country air and took their culinary act to Atlanta, on the northern edge of Hamilton County. The Boyds moved into a tall, narrow brick building on Main Street, and Indianapolis devotees soon became accustomed to driving out to Atlanta to feast on seasonally changing, innovative renditions of fresh fish, chicken breasts, beef tenderloin, veal, and lamb. All of this is detailed in a truly amusing menu in which a dinner item may bear the title "Footprints in Red," and such game as venison, elk, and ostrich come under the heading "Fletcher's Road Kill," followed by the explanation, "What treasures of the tarmac our peripatetic souls find, we share with you." And in the summer and fall, should you find the mildly convoluted directions to Fletcher's baffling, you can hop on a weekend train from Fishers, provided by the Indiana Transportation Museum, for a special dinner package at Fletcher's of Atlanta. Fletcher's success as a remote outpost of dining excellence seems to have inspired other young chefs to pursue their culinary muse in the hinterlands, on the theory: "If you cook it, and cook it well, they will come."

Kona Jack's Fish Market & Sushi Bar
INDIANAPOLIS

9413 N. Meridian Street   (317) 843-1609

1 N. Pennsylvania Street   (317) 822-3474

Open for lunch and dinner Monday–Saturday

Restaurant entrepreneur Jim Thompson, after a rousing success with his restaurant-pub, Daddy Jack's, in an Indianapolis strip mall off 96th and North Meridian streets, took to the sea in 1992 by establishing a fresh seafood mecca next door called Kona Jack's. As the name might suggest, the bulk of Kona Jack's seabeasts formerly cruised the shores of Hawaii in the Pacific. Thus, the menu showcases the dolphinfish, mahi-mahi; the silky textured escolar; the meaty "ahi-ahi" yellowfin tuna; "onaga" red snapper; and aku swordfish, along with more familiar Atlantic and lake contributions such as grouper, salmon, scrod, trout, walleyed pike, and Arctic char. All can be rendered grilled, sautéed, or blackened. The nautically themed main dining room features a full-service fish market so you can try all this at home, and an adjoining sushi bar at which to revel in raw seafood. In 1999, Thompson opened a downtown outpost of Kona Jack's at the northeast corner of Washington and Pennyslvania streets.

LaSalle Grill
SOUTH BEND

115 W. Colfax Ave.   (219)288-1155/ (800) 382-9323

Open for dinner Monday–Saturday

Housed in an 1865-vintage structure in downtown South Bend that was once the LaSalle Hotel, the LaSalle Grill was opened in the spring of 1991 by Mark McDonnell as a fine-dine forum for nouvelle American cuisine. The menu changes daily to reflect the gourmet whims of the kitchen staff. The fish of the evening could be fresh tilapia or mahi-mahi; on the turf side the offerings might be rack of lamb, prime steaks, and pan-seared duck breast. McDonnell has just opened a jazz club upstairs called Club LaSalle, along with a classy bar with an area for the puffing of Perfectos and other fine-tobacco success symbols.

Le Petit Café
BLOOMINGTON

308 W. 6th Street   (812) 334-9747

Open for lunch and dinner Monday–Sunday

French-born Patrick Fiore was attending Indiana University on a Fulbright scholarship in music in 1977 when he and his Italian-born wife, Marina, decided to open a small café in an old two-story structure in the historic Levee section of Bloomington. Before long they were compelled to use both floors to accommodate customers enamored of the continental passion which Marina lavished on imaginative menus that changed daily. Nearly a quarter of a century later, the passions remain fully stoked with Marina's creative approaches to veal, beef, lamb, chicken, fresh fish, and even rabbit, combining her inspirations with both Gallic and Italiano charm.

Loon Lake Lodge
INDIANAPOLIS

6880 E. 82nd Street   (317) 845-9011

Open for lunch and dinner every day

Loon Lake Lodge is one of the more colorful restaurants to enter the Indianapolis dining landscape in recent years. Chip and Rick Laughner, in 1998, transformed one of their family's largest cafeterias in the Castleton area into something reminiscent of the remote mountain resorts of yore, where wealthy businessmen would send their families to escape the city's summer heat, and join them on weekends—hence such wilderness touches as early-morning fog effects, animatronic denizens of the forest flitting and lumbering about, and an eye-catching Cessna 152 seaplane perched on the roof. The menu continues the theme with free-range rotisserie chicken; prime steaks and prime rib; such wild game selections as venison, elk, pheasant, and buffalo; line-caught fresh salmon, walleye, and trout; and barbecued ribs. Just look for the sign of the Cessna.

Majestic Restaurant
INDIANAPOLIS

47 S. Pennsylvania Street   (317) 636-5418

Open for lunch and dinner Monday–Saturday

Donal Weaving opened this downtown restaurant as the Majestic Oyster Bar & Grille in 1983 in the historic 1895 Majestic Building, Indianapolis' first steel-skeleton structure, designed by Oscar D. Bohlen for the Indianapolis Gas Company. Later, chef Weaving shortened the name to the Majestic to reflect a wide-ranging menu of creatively prepared prime steaks, fresh seafood, and such signature entrées as Steak Olympia—lobster slices on New York strip; baked crabmeat-stuffed shrimp; lemon sole; South African lobster tails; and veal and lobster fettuccine. Marbled walls and Corinthian columns make for one of downtown's classiest dining experiences.

Mama Carolla's Old Italian Restaurant
INDIANAPOLIS

1031 E. 54th Street   (317) 259-9412

Open for dinner Tuesday–Saturday

Mama Carolla's is tucked into Indianapolis' northside Meridian-Kessler neighborhood in a 1920s Spanish-style stucco structure that served as a residence for most of its existence until Carole and Howard Leuer turned it into an Italian restaurant, with recipes collected from prominent Italian eateries at a prior port of call—Omaha, Nebraska. The Leuers achieved quick success with their creative array of pastas, notably the chicken rigatoni, manicotti stuffed with ricotta cheese, ravioli, and lasagna, and a mix of veal, fresh fish, and chicken dishes, most notably the roasted rosemary chicken and the yellowfin tuna in marinara sauce. The restaurant is laid out in two levels full of cozy dining nooks, with an attractive courtyard for alfresco dining sometime after the spring thaw.

Michael's Uptown Café
BLOOMINGTON

102 E. Kirkwood Avenue   (812) 339-0900

Open for breakfast, lunch, and dinner Monday–Saturday,
breakfast and lunch Sunday

Michael Cassidy and Bill Hittner opened their Uptown Café in 1976 as a cozy breakfast and lunch place on Walnut Street in downtown Bloomington. In 1986, Cassidy acceded to the pleas of its growing and glowing clientele for more elbow room in which to wolf down Uptown's celebrated power omelettes, creative pancakes, and innovative sandwiches and salads. About a block south and just east of the Square, he established a roomier bistro, adding an array of spicy dinner fare sporting a detectable Cajun accent: jambalayas, gumbos, blackened seafood and beef, along with specials stressing fresh ingredients and in-season produce and herbs. And the power breakfasts still prevail, especially for weekend schmoozing.

Midtown Grill
INDIANAPOLIS

815 E. Westfield Boulevard   (317) 253-1141

Open for lunch and dinner daily

Since entering the Broad Ripple neighborhood dining pool in 1986, the Midtown Grill has offered some of the city's most eclectic and innovative dishes, thanks to Egyptian-born Hamada Ibrahim. Its original location was on Broad Ripple Avenue; now it has more spacious digs a block north, allowing room for warm-weather alfresco dining. But indoors or out, Midtown Grill has won consistent kudos for the likes of walnut-crusted rack of lamb; filet mignon in Dijon mustard sauce, flamed tableside; grilled swordfish and blackened New York strip; salmon Wellington (salmon and artichokes baked in puff pastry); and grilled chicken breasts topped in spicy chipotle-black bean sauce. In 1998, Ibrahim gave that same eclectic touch to Lulu's Restaurant (8487 Union Chapel Road, off East 86th and Keystone Avenue, [317] 251-5858), in the southern wing of Keystone at the Crossing.

Peter's—A Restaurant and Bar
INDIANAPOLIS

8505 Keystone Crossing Boulevard   (317) 465-1155

Open for dinner, Monday–Saturday

Peter George came down to Indianapolis from the South Bend area in 1985 to make his mark as one of the state's most innovative restaurateurs with the opening of Peter's on Virginia Avenue, immediately south of downtown. Housed in a modest wooden structure with minimalist decor, directly across from the regional headquarters of White Castle Hamburgers, Peter's built and secured a loyal clientele in introducing under young chef Tony Hanslits the concept of seasonally changing menus of American regional cuisine, stressing fresh foods and in-season herbs, seasonings, and ingredients. The bulk of his clientele were northsiders, and George eventually caved in to their persistent nagging and moved just south of Keystone at the Crossing to a restaurant and kitchen he designed himself. His wide-ranging menu continues to dazzle his constituency with the likes of marinated leg of lamb, twice-roasted Indiana duckling, free-range chicken, New Zealand venison, steak Diane. Most of these dishes are also available in smaller portions for those who just came from the health spa.

Peter's Bay
COLUMBUS

310 Commons Mall   (812) 372-2270

Open for lunch, Monday–Friday, for dinner, Monday–Saturday

Marty and Barbara Pittman opened Peter's Bay in the Commons Shopping Mall in downtown Columbus in 1990 as a culinary tribute to the sultans of the sea—fresh coldwater fish—complete with a small retail fish market off the foyer. They sold Peter's Bay in 1992 to the current owners, Gary and Debbie Garber, who added sushi to the proceedings, augmenting a menu revolving around fresh Atlantic salmon, yellowfin tuna, escolar, mahi-mahi, Boston sole, and tilapia. Such shell beasts as clams, oysters, scallops, mussels, and shrimp also achieve star billing, with a line of steaks, chicken, and pasta dishes for a change of pace.

Restaurant 210
CARMEL

210 N. Rangeline Road   (317) 582-1414

Open for lunch and dinner Monday–Saturday

In 1997, chef Mike Myers, another of the cadre of youthful chefs breaking out to casual fine-dine independence, took over a two-story vintage-1900 residence to show off his abundant culinary skills. Myers put great stress on the fresh fish specials on his seasonally, and sometimes monthly, changing menus. Frequently highlighted are braised lamb and veal shanks, mushroom ravioli in Roquefort sauce, pork medallions glazed in sautéed apples, brandy, and apple butter, seared duck breast, and seared sea scallops. It is like having dinner in the home of good friends, with the friends doing the cooking and cleaning up afterwards.

Restaurant at the Canterbury
INDIANAPOLIS

Canterbury Hotel/ 123 S. Illinois Street
(317) 634-2000, extension 7230

Open for breakfast, lunch, and dinner every day; afternoon tea every day, 4 P.M.–5:30 P.M.

The Canterbury Hotel opened in all its refurbished splendor from the remnants of the old Warren Hotel in 1985 as downtown's most prominent luxury hotel. Under the tutelage of its master European chef, Volker Rudolph (not Rudolph Volker, as many patrons who know him best as "Chef Rudy" incorrectly assume), the small, clubby dining room quickly emerged as one of the city's most compelling dining experiences, with Chef Rudy's lavish renditions of Dover sole, herb-crusted rack of lamb, veal chops, roast Indiana duckling, Black Angus filets, and sautéed lobster and veal medallions in a sherry cream sauce. As the Restaurant at the Canterbury, it is open for breakfast and lunch, and is the only downtown restaurant to offer afternoon tea.

Shaffer's Restaurant
INDIANAPOLIS

6100 N. Keystone Avenue   (317) 253-1404

Open for lunch Monday–Friday; for dinner, Monday–Saturday

Over the years since their 1977 opening on Keystone Avenue across from the Glendale Shopping Mall on Indianapolis' northeastside, brothers Greg and Glen Shaffer developed a reputation for their fondue dinners, inviting diners to dip chunks of beef, chicken, shrimp, lobster, scallops, and other seafood into hot oil. Cheese and chocolate fondues are also featured. It's been particularly nostalgic for couples married in the '70s who received seven fondue pots as shower or wedding presidents, but wound up putting them in storage in deference to the speed and efficiency of the microwave. Recently the Shaffers took their menu to new levels with a wide array of fresh seafood, Black Angus beef, Atlantic rock lobster tails, and such specialty items as center cut pork loin chops, smoked Boston bluefish, and filet of ostrich. For the record, the ostrich tastes not like chicken, but like lean roast beef, and commendably so. With the untimely death of Greg Shaffer in June 2000 the Indiana restaurant community lost one of its most innovative members.

Something Different & Snax
INDIANAPOLIS

4939 E. 82nd Street   (317) 570-7700

Open for dinner Monday–Saturday

Something Different was first launched in the mid-'80s by Susan and Drew Goss off East 65th and Keystone Avenue to display their artistic and creative preparations and presentations of gourmet regional American cuisine, joined at the hip to a more casual bar and restaurant called Snax that specialized in innovative appetizers. In the early '90s the Gosses left to open the acclaimed Zinfandel Restaurant in Chicago, turning Something Different and Snax over to chef Tony Hanslits, formerly of Peter's. Hanslits maintained their lofty reputation while contributing something different from his repertoire to place it high on assorted best Indy restaurant lists, but departed in the summer of 1997 to become chef of Carmel's Woodland Country Club. His protégé, Steven Oakley, took control, moving Something Different and Snax to tonier digs in the bustling Clearwater area west of Castleton. Something Different continues to be acclaimed for the artistry and architectural dazzle of its monthly changing dishes, with more pasta dishes and such entrées as cider pepper-glazed pork chops, Chilean sea bass poached in olive oil, grilled and braised pheasant, and duck breast in Peking spice glaze, all garnished so beautifully with accompanying vegetables and herbs that diners are briefly reluctant to apply knife and fork to these works of art.

Ye Olde Library
CARMEL

40 E. Main Street   (317) 573-4444

Open for lunch and dinner Tuesday–Saturday

Taking a cue from Carnegie's in Greenfield, Kevin Rider purchased an old Carnegie library that had been lying fallow after many decades of impeccable literary service to the scholars of Carmel. Enlisting chefs Michael Todd Harmon and Tim Mally, two young disciples of the Glass Chimney's Dieter Puska, Rider opened the Ye Olde Library in 1998, with two cozy book-lined dining rooms and an extensive menu of American regional cuisine that changes daily but that might well feature Black Angus beef, lamb, pork tenderloin, veal, and at least four fresh fish dishes. On a given night, diners may curl up with a rib-eye in a whiskey glaze; arctic char and yellow-tail snapper; beef medallions with sautéed oyster mushrooms in Madeira wine sauce; and hickory-smoked pork tenderloin in a honey-mustard sauce. This is still another bistro unleashing young culinary talent and offering the full gourmet experience by keeping it small, focused, casual, distinctive, creative, at prices that can pass for reasonable under the most pleasant circumstances.

INDEX

Restaurants

Acapulco Joe's Mexican Restaurant, 1
Adam's Rib & Seafood House, 116
Agio, 117
Amalfi Ristorante, 117
Ambrosia, 118
Amici's Ristorante, 118
Anvil Inn, 96
Arturo's, 119

Bando, 114
Bangkok Restaurant, 115
Bay Window, 77
Bazbeaux Pizza, 78
Beef House, 4
Bobby Joe's Beef and Brew, 97
Bonge's Tavern, 119
Brandywine Steakhouse, 98
Broad Ripple Brewpub, 78
Broad Ripple Steakhouse, 98
Bynum's Steak House, 99

Café Johnell, 6
Carnegie's, 120
Central House, 121
Chalkie's Restaurant and Billiards, 79
Chan's Garden, 103
Chanteclair, 9
Chez Jean, 11
Classic Kitchen, 121
Corner Wine Bar, 122
Country Cook Inn, 79

Daruma, 111
Das Dutchman Essenhaus, 13
Delafield's, 80
Different Drummer, 122
Dodd's Townhouse, 16
Dunaway's Palazzo Ossigeno, 123

Eagle's Nest, 124
Edwards Drive-in, 80
El Sol de Tala, 110

Fiddlers Three, 124
Fireside South, 99
Fletcher's of Atlanta, 124
Forbidden City, 104
Foxfires, 18
Frank and Mary's, 81

Ginza Japanese Steak House, 113
Glass Chimney, 21
Gray Brothers Cafeteria, 23
G.T. South's Rib House, 82

Haub House, 100
Hellas Cafe, 107
Hollyhock Hill, 25
Hong Kong Inn, 104

Iaria's Italian Restaurant, 27
India Garden, 110
India Palace, 111

Indianapolis City Market, 82
Irish Lion, 109
Iron Skillet, 29
Ivanhoe's, 83

Janko's Little Zagreb, 31
Jazz Cooker, 84
Jonathan Byrd's Cafeteria, 84

Kabul, 107
Knobby's Restaurant, 85
Kona Jack's Fish Market & Sushi Bar, 125
Kopper Kettle Inn, 34
Korey's, 108

LaSalle Grill, 126
Laughner's Cafeteria, 86
Lemon Drop, 86
Le Petit Café, 126
Little Zagreb, Janko's, 31
Log Inn, 37
Loon Lake Lodge, 127
Louie's Coney Island, 87

Majestic Restaurant, 127
Mama Carolla's Old Italian Restaurant, 128
MaMa's House, 114
Maple Corner Restaurant, 40
Mayberry Café, 88
MCL Cafeteria, 88
Michael's Uptown Café, 128
Midtown Grill, 129
Mikado, 113
Milano Inn, 42
Mug n' Bun Drive-in, 89

Nashville House, 45
New Ross Steak House, 101
Nick's Chili Parlor, 90
Nick's English Hut, 90

Overlook Restaurant, 47

Pa & Ma's Barbecue, 91
Parthenon, 108
Peter's—A Restaurant and Bar, 129
Peter's Bay, 130
Phil Smidt's, 49

Queen of Sheba, 106

Rathskeller, 106
Red Dog Steakhouse, 101
Red Geranium, 52
Restaurant 210, 130
Restaurant at the Canterbury, 131
Russia House, 115

Sahm's Restaurant, 91
St. Elmo Steak House, 54
Sakura, 112
Sakura Ocean Grill, 112
Sarge Oak on Main, 57
Shaffers' Restaurant, 131
Shapiro's Delicatessen, 60
Sol de Tala, El, 110
Solly's, 102
Some Guys Pasta and Pizza Grill, 92
Something Different & Snax, 132
Story Inn, 64
Strongbow Turkey Inn, 67

Teibel's Restaurant, 70
Tippecanoe Place, 72
Triple XXX Drive-In, 93

Welliver's Smorgasbord, 75
Wolf's Barb-B-Cue, 93
Workingman's Friend, 94

Ye Olde Library, 133
Yen Ching, 105

Zydeco's New Orleans Grill, 95

Recipes

Apple Dumplings (Das Dutchman Essenhaus), 15
Apple Pie, Country (Maple Corner), 42

Banana-Walnut Pancakes (Story Inn), 66
Beets, Pickled (Iron Skillet), 31
Biscuits (Das Dutchman Essenhaus), 16

Biscuits, Fried (Nashville House), 46
Bleu Cheese-Dill Dressing (Story Inn), 66
Bleu Cheese Dressing (Beef House), 6
Broccoli Cheddar Soup (Little Zagreb), 33
Broccoli Soup (Beef House), 5
Brownies (Iron Skillet), 30
Buttermilk Pie (Dodd's Townhouse), 18

Cabbage, Stuffed (Shapiro's Deli), 62
Caesar Salad (Chanteclair), 10
Caesar Steak (Red Geranium), 54
Cannoli Filling (Iaria's), 29
Celery Seed Dressing (Sarge Oak), 59
Cheddar Mashed Redskins (St. Elmo), 56
Cheese Ball (Welliver's), 76
Cheesecake (Log Inn), 39–40
Cheesecake, Smoked Salmon (Foxfires), 20
Chicken, Country, Golden Pan-Fried (Kopper Kettle), 37
Chicken, Creamed (Overlook Restaurant), 49
Chicken Liver Pâté (Café Johnell), 8
Chicken Piccata (Milano Inn), 44
Chocolate Amaretto Pie (Sarge Oak), 59
Chocolate Chip Pie (Dodd's Townhouse), 18
Chocolate Torte, Flourless (Shapiro's Deli), 63
Cindy's Cole Slaw (Hollyhock Hill), 26
Cindy's Salad (Hollyhock Hill), 26
Cole Slaw (Nashville House), 46
Cole Slaw, Cindy's (Hollyhock Hill), 26
Coq au Vin (Tippecanoe Place), 74
Country Apple Pie (Maple Corner), 42
Country Chicken, Golden Pan-fried (Kopper Kettle Inn), 36
Country Green Beans (Kopper Kettle Inn), 36
Creamed Chicken (Overlook Restaurant), 49
Creamed Spinach (St. Elmo), 57
Cream of Onion Soup (Welliver's), 76
Crème Brûlée (Chez Jean), 13
Crème Caramel (Glass Chimney), 23

Dressing, Bleu Cheese-Dill (Story Inn), 66
Dressing, Celery Seed (Sarge Oak), 59

Eggpant Provolone (Little Zagreb), 33

Farfalle with Sausage & Leeks (Milano Inn), 44
Fettuccine Alfredo (Iaria's), 28
Flourless Chocolate Torte (Shapiro's Deli), 63
French Dressing (Overlook Restaurant), 49
Fried Biscuits (Nashville House), 46
Fried Chicken (Kopper Kettle Inn), 37

Grace Ann's Chocolate Amaretto Pie (Sarge Oak), 59
Grand Marnier Sauce (Cafe Johnell), 8
Green Beans, Country (Kopper Kettle Inn), 36

Lemon Pie, Shaker (Red Geranium), 54
Lobster, Grilled (Phil Smidt's), 51

Margaritas (Maple Corner), 42
Mushroom Caps, Stuffed (Teibel's), 71

Nashville House Cole Slaw, 46
Nashville House Fried Biscuits, 46

Onion Soup, Cream of (Welliver's), 76

Pancakes, Banana-Walnut (Story Inn), 66
Pecan Pie, Southern (Tippecanoe Place), 74
Pie, Buttermilk (Dodd's Townhouse), 18
Pie, Chocolate Amaretto (Sarge Oak), 59
Pie, Chocolate Chip (Dodd's Townhouse), 18
Pie, Country Apple (Maple Corner), 42
Pie, Fresh Strawberry (Log Inn), 40
Pie, Shaker Lemon (Red Geranium), 54
Pie, Southern Pecan (Tippecanoe Place), 74
Pickled Beets (Iron Skillet), 31
Pinto Beans (Phil Smidt's), 52
Pork Chops, Rum-Mango Glazed (Foxfires), 19

Pork Tenderloin Medallions (Chez Jean), 12

Salad, Cindy's (Hollyhock Hill), 26
Sausage Gravy, Hot (Acapulco Joe's), 3
Shaker Lemon Pie (Red Geranium), 54
Soup, Broccoli (Beef House), 5
Soup, Broccoli Cheddar (Little Zagreb), 33
Soup, Cream of Onion (Welliver's), 76
Soup, Turkey (Strongbow Inn), 69
Soup, Veal, Viennese-style (Glass Chimney), 22
Southern Pecan Pie (Tippecanoe Place), 74

Spinach, Creamed (St. Elmo), 57
Steak, Caesar (Red Geranium), 54
Steak Diane (Chanteclair), 10
Strawberry Pie, Fresh (Log Inn), 40
Stuffed Cabbage (Shapiro's Deli), 62
Stuffed Mushroom Caps (Teibel's), 71

Taco Filling (Acapulco Joe's), 3
Turkey à la King (Strongbow Inn), 69
Turkey Soup (Strongbow Inn), 69

Veal Soup Viennese-style (Glass Chimney), 22

Wiener Kalbseinmach Suppe, 22

Reid Duffy has worked since 1971 as a television news reporter, teacher, humor writer, and restaurant and film reviewer for WRTV and WNDY in Indianapolis. He was the host of "Duffy's Diner," a television show that reviewed various eating establishments. He is the author of *Indianapolis Dining* (1981) and coauthor with Mike Ahern of a novel, *Festerwood at Five: A "Novel" Approach to TV News*. He lives in Indianapolis with his wife and children.